WHAT MAKES YOU THINK
WE READ THE BILLS?

WHAT MAKES YOU THINK WE READ THE BILLS?

Senator H. L. "Bill" Richardson

Foreword by Mark Russell

CAROLINE HOUSE BOOKS / Green Hill Publishers, Inc.

Ottawa, Illinois

WHAT MAKES YOU THINK WE READ THE BILLS?

Copyright © 1978 by H. L. Richardson

Library of Congress Catalogue Card Number: 78-66391

Manufactured in the United States of America
ISBN: 0-916054-78-0

CONTENTS

Foreword by Mark Russell 5

Preface 7

1. Show Biz 9
2. The Nature of the Job 12
3. Instant Smart 16
4. Gangrene and the Board of Education 19
5. Legislators: A Most Pleasant Lot 23
6. What's A Seat Worth? 28
7. Read the Bills! 36
8. 200 Secrets 47
9. Burros and the Pill 53
10. Intellectuals They Are Not 61
11. Who Says It's Fair? 64
12. Peer-Group Shift 68
13. Too Many Lawyers 73
14. Restitution, Regulation, and Redistribution 79
15. A Full Time Legislature—Yuk! 90
16. Ze Mooz 95
17. Ancient Origins of Lobbying 107
18. The Majority Elects? 112
19. The Pot Shoot 120
20. The God Demos 124
21. Sexy Solons 130
22. God Alone 134

FOREWORD

BILL RICHARDSON is a menace.

Quick! Deport him! Abort him!

God help politicians and political humorists if anyone ever clones him.

We've had a good thing going until now. Political jackasses of all types—grinning idiots who agree with everyone and please no one; sourpuss ideologues from places like cambridge, Mass., Whittier, Calif., Madison, Wisc., and Montgomery, Ala.; assorted mutations of the above—and we political humorists have been living in strato-porcine proximity (federalese for high off the hog).

It's been *fun* making sport of these fellows, and *they've* had a grand time at the legislative trough. No one's been the wiser.

Until now.

Richardson has let the cat out of the bag, boys. And probably shortened my career by decades. I'm going to lose all my material!

They say every American mania starts in California. Rock and roll, Red-baiting, dope, skateboards, hippies, hot tubs and Zen politics, Black Panthers and vote yourself a $1000-cut-in real estate taxes. And now, from Arcadia, California, comes one Senator Richardson: straight talk and sass. Is America ready for a laughing apostle of Truth-in-Politics?

I dunno. We transcended H. L. Mencken, who was wont to toss off such zingers as "nothing is so abject and pathetic as a politician who has lost his job, save only a retired stud horse." Mark Twain and Will Rogers came and went, leaving chuckles in their wakes, but politics went on as usual. I suppose Art Buchwald best summed up what's happened to us when he

5

said recently, "I used to be a liberal . . . Now I don't know what I am. I'm suspicious of big government and I don't think they can solve any of the problems. Like most people, I thought government was the solution. Now I think it's the problem."

If Bill Richardson's zany tales from the legislature are not peculiar to California, and I fear they are not, then you can put me down as Chairman of the Committee to Keep the Three Martini Lunch.

Fun's fun. Kidding the pols has made a great career for me. *But these guys mean business!* And the lobbyists who yank their chains aren't pulling down a hundred grand a year for nothing.

Milton Friedman said a few years ago that most laws get passed because of "people who want to do good and people who want to do well." Well, Lord love the do-gooders, but as Bill Richardson shows, you'd better keep your eyes on those other fellows.

Read this book. It's full of grand yarns—you'll even learn why all the urinals in Sacramento turned blue a few years back. But more important in this day of "lowered expectations" from government, the book gives you the bottom line in government today, in lurid detail. For many, it will mark the beginning of political wisdom.

As for me, I stand with Mencken: "We live in a land of abounding quackeries, and if we do not learn how to laugh we succumb to the melancholy disease which afflicts the race of viewers-with-alarm. I have had too good a time of it to go down that chute."

Washington, D.C.   MARK RUSSELL

PREFACE

A NUMBER OF YEARS ago, some sage group proclaimed that amongst state legislatures, California was numero uno—number one. I must admit my ego was properly massaged since I happen to be one of the anointed who serve in the California Senate. A smug look adorned my countenance as I read the article praising me and my colleagues. Then all of a sudden it hit me—"Good Lord! If we're number one, the other forty-nine states are in real trouble!"

I've been a full-time California State legislator for twelve years. The longer I watch the legislature in action, the more I'm convinced that we're part of the problem rather than the solution. I think it is fair to say I know a little bit about public representatives' public, and private lives. I have associated with hundreds of solons from California, other states, and Washington, D. C. I understand the legislative process, the problems, and the people who comprise the legislature—not as an outsider but as an insider. I am privy to what goes on in the back rooms of the legislative chambers.

The American legislative process is fundamentally the same across America. The procedure may change somewhat from state to state or in the U.S. House and Senate. The rules each legislature uses will vary but the basic format is the same. One ingredient never changes, the legislator himself.

Legislators are people. Unfortunately, the power the electorate gives them does nothing to make them brighter, wiser or fairer than anyone else. The only difference is that, when elected, they acquire power over others and their human frail-

7

ties sometimes become magnified because of the power they acquire. We have a lot of well-meaning humans bumbling around the legislative halls of America, trying to bring human happiness by passing laws, and as humans, they have legislated a mountain of agencies, commissions, and bureaus filled with -crats.

Maybe this book can throw a little humorous light on a most serious subject and show why seeking freedom from our own elected governments is the best path to take. Our forefathers groaned about taxation without representation. Today we groan about something worse—taxation with representation!

1

Show Biz

Believe it or not, a lot of people think legislators are big time stuff. Although politicians are condemned in general, they are given great respect in person. Maybe one of the reasons is because most folks rarely get their names in the newspapers or appear on T.V., so anyone who is constantly in the media gains some celebrity status. Like folks in show biz, politicians can be minor-to-major grade celebrities. U.S. Senators Goldwater and Kennedy deserve star billing and people treat them as such. The bigger the name the greater the awe from the general public. Politics and show biz do have a lot in common—both deal in make-believe, and both conjure up images of the impossible. *Star Wars* and the Congress deal with the outer limits of credibility—with *Star Wars* the more believable of the two. Theatrical and political ham tastes much the same.

Whether we deserve it or not, public adoration occasionally graces our legislative abodes.

Not too long ago, my secretary ushered in a constituent and his family; you would have thought they were being ushered into the presence of God. I haven't the foggiest notion what the father told the three children, but the whole family came in with their eyes wide and their mouths agape. They were all five huddled close together and seemed to enter my office in unison. From out of the pack shot the father's hand.

"Senator Richardson," he meekly smiled, "I'm Mr.

Sooooo, honored to meet you. The family and I are on vacation and we thought we would stop by and see the Capitol. We saw your office and stopped in. We *never*, *ever* thought we would have a chance to meet you. We're *so* honored!"

Situations like this are sort of embarrassing to me. I never feel quite up to the occasion and usually feel nervous. Obviously they think a Senator is big stuff and my tendency is to want, at least momentarily, to live up to their image. At times like this I wish I could levitate. It would be all so simple. All I would have to do is rise a few inches off the floor and carry on small talk. Everybody would be so happy and properly impressed. Unfortunately, politicians can't rise an inch above the desk no matter how many bills we might pass mandating legislative levitation; politicians' feet reach all the way to the floor just like everyone else's. Take it from me, we are not miracle workers—maybe junior-grade celebrities—but men blessed with supreme power we're not.

The world has a lot of people who try to do impossible things. Not too long ago a man packed his 80-year-old mother in ice after she had physically and spiritually departed from this world. He sincerely believed he could raise her from the dead. For 13 days he tried but Mama had departed and wasn't coming back!

Gurus in India are constantly trying to levitate. Somehow they just don't make it. The laws of gravity have yet to be repealed and no matter how long the gurus grunt, or fast, or meditate, their bottoms have yet to clear the deck.

I'm not saying that miracles can't happen because I'm sure they can. God can miraculously heal and I'm sure if He wanted He could levitate the whole of India, cows and all. Divine intervention can perform the impossible, but the last time I looked, the legislature had no direct pipeline to the Lord. Outside of cursory acknowledgment before each session, prayer is noted by its absence.

Miracles are not the prerogative of state or federal legislatures. We are most assuredly not divine. We, in all of our imagined might, can't conjure up one teensy-weensy clap of thunder. All the majority votes in the world can't bring one drop of rain. Not one of us has ever risen after death no matter how high we have climbed in public office, nor has one politician ever been nominated for sainthood.

Why then, since divinity is not our bag, do people expect us to accomplish the impossible? Why do people expect us to heal the sick, provide shelter, create national and state well-being, and mandate equality by legislative decree?

All of the above cost money. Since we cannot create real wealth or tranquility by magic or by waving the majority vote wand, whatever we do financially must come from someone who already has earned income. We then are not agents of magic, but agents of transfer. We transfer from the haves to the wants and sic revenue agents on those who won't respond to our demands. Nothing magical in that, that's just old fashioned plunder, legitimatized by majority vote.

Money and power are volatile ingredients. Once you concentrate either into the hands of men, expect all of their frailties to be sorely tested. If both money and power reside in the hands of a few men, expect them to be courted, curried, complimented and cajoled by everyone who wants to be the beneficiary of their power and wealth. Saints are needed to withstand the temptations of the flesh but, alas, saints we're not.

I know none of my colleagues have extraordinary powers. No one could *Shazam*! up a ham sandwich on a night when we were debating late into the evening.

Wait a second though . . . now that I remember, we *did* make a lot of tax dollars disappear.

2

The Nature of the Job

CHARLIE SLUMPED cockeyed in the chair before my desk with his legs crossed, his right arm dangling over the chair arm while his left arm waved aimlessly in the air.

"Bill, have you ever seen the country in worse shape? Well, have you?" Before I could answer, my friend Charlie droned on. "The country's morals are going to pot. I tell you, with inflation, corruption, oil shortages, Watergate, and hanky-panky in high office, whom can you trust?"

"Well, ah. . . ," I started to reply, but before I could get my jaw moving, he answered himself.

"Nobody, that's who—they're all a bunch of no-account, rotten bums. You bust your lower back getting them into office and they all go south on you!"

Charlie looked at me and realized that standing before him was one of the "bums" he had helped elect. The blood rushed to his face, turning it to a beautiful sunset blush. "Oh, er, gag, present company excluded . . . but . . ." Charlie dejectedly slumped deeper into his chair and deeper into despair.

My friend felt betrayed, not once, but many times. He had supported his party, walked precincts, donated money, and adorned his family's car with bumper stickers that he knew would come off somewhere around the year 2000.

He had financially backed candidates he knew had only a slight chance of victory and even some with no chance at all. Charlie had given his time, money, and enthusiasm; the only thing he hadn't done was run for office himself.

12

Charlie dejectedly pulled himself from his seat and headed toward the door mumbling, "I thought they were good men. What went wrong?"

Charlie was in no mood to listen. Without waiting for an answer he shuffled out of my office mumbling, "What's the use? This coming election I think I'll go fishing."

Story sound familiar? It should. The sequel, in its many different forms, has been played over and over in the last decade. People are turned off by politics in general and politicians in particular. Politicians are as popular as Liberace at a rock concert or a Salvation Army band providing the jiggle music at a Bunny Club.

I think it is fair to say that a sizable number of Americans are disturbed over the direction our nation has taken, and they aren't too happy with the results of contemporary politics. Who is to blame? Who should get the heat? Politicians?

I'm not one to agree that politicos don't deserve their fair share of the blame, but I'm convinced the problem is greater than just the quality of men we elect.

I believe the major hangup is that we have completely forgotten the job description of what an American politician is supposed to do. We have concentrated too much on the character and personality of the candidate and have misunderstood the task which we have assigned to our elected leaders.

The character of the candidate is important, but *the nature of the task to be performed* is infinitely more so. The public has blithely asked its elected officeholders to do the impossible and, unfortunately, those who seek office have been dumb enough to try it. Let me give you an example.

What if Bob Hope were enlisted as the state hangman? The nature of his job is to hang people—pure and simple. He would probably be more jovial in the performance of his task, but it would not change the function of his job. Put a humorless man in charge of the same job, and the nature of the job will not change one whit.

The nature of the job is making dead people out of live ones. A jolly necktie artist might get a chuckle out of the jailer, but it wouldn't change the function of his job. Nor could the hanger evoke many yuks from the hangee. Hangings just aren't funny. Once you have accepted the premise that you need a gallows, rope, and trapdoor, and a hangman to spring the trap, the personal character and morality of the hangman become secondary.

In contemporary politics we have stressed the importance of honesty, morality, and ethics in our political personalities and have been naive in what we have wanted these honest, moral, and ethical personalities to do once elected.

The point is, the character of a politician may well be irrelevant unless, first, it is established exactly what is expected of him.

Here is where I believe we have gone astray. I am convinced the job description of politics that Americans now accept is so broad, so ill defined, so all-encompassing, that no group of perfect men could ever perform under the best of circumstances.

Americans expect their elected leaders to do three things: 1. Legislate solutions to all social problems. 2. Fairly redistribute the wealth in order to accomplish (1) above. 3. Impose government regulations wherever government sees fit to do so.

This is what I believe Americans have come to accept as their governmental job description. No wonder everything is so screwed up. Politicians are asked to play God, and, unfortunately, too many of them think they can.

I hope to show you in this book why elected officials cannot redistribute the wealth equitably, plan intelligently, legislate fairly, or regulate without bias. They are human, and as their nature prescribes, they act accordingly.

I hope my thoughts will provide an interesting and humorous insight into both the mechanics and the people who serve in our contemporary system of governmental madness. I think you will find that what happens in California eventually, for better or worse, happens elsewhere. Although many people think California has an inordinate share of nutty people, you may be assured that the legislative goobers are scattered in every state.

3

Instant Smart

FOR SOME mystic reason, people believe that elections confer upon the elected "instant smart"—wisdom beyond their years and beyond their peers—as if sudden knowledge were infused into the mind of the anointed via ballot.

When I first ran for election to the state senate, one town in my district proved to be a particularly tough one to crack. Leading citizens viewed me as a young upstart, a newcomer to the political scene, untested, untried, and untrusted. My views were received with skepticism on those rare occasions when I had the opportunity to present them.

I was not invited into the inner circle of the socially accepted, even after I had handily won the primary. I was just another aspirant to public office, one of the many whose characteristics were easily recognized—the glad hand and perpetual smile . . . a fistful of literature . . . seeking campaign contributions. But I never made it into the inner sanctum until the day after I was elected.

Then I was quickly offered the opportunity to address the "in" service club in town. I was greeted and feted like a newly arrived potentate.

"Congratulations on your victory, senator."

"Smashing win, senator."

"I'm sure glad *we* won, senator."

"Senator, I am so-and-so, and would like you to meet some of your strongest supporters . . . ."

"The head table is right this way, senator."

16

"We are all looking forward to what you have to say."

What a difference a day made. November 3 I was candidate What's-his-name. November 4 I was Senator Big Deal, himself.

I gave them my hell-and-brimstone, series A516, speech. That's the one where I tell them we are all going to hell if our state doesn't recognize the good guys and throw out the bad guys. I had to change some phrases from "when I win, we will" to "now that we have won, we are going to . . ." But the speech was basically the same one I had been giving throughout the campaign.

What was viewed with skepticism on November 3 became gospel truth on November 4. I must admit, I was in fine form and received a standing ovation. I had arrived.

After the meeting adjourned, many came forward to congratulate me on my speech and to ask questions.

"Senator, what do you think about the fiscal solvency of our state retirement policies?"

"What is your opinion, senator, on tenure of university regents?"

"Senator, the marketing orders on agricultural products are getting repressive. What should we do about it?"

"The business inventory tax needs readjustment, senator. What is the senate or the administration going to do about it?"

I didn't have the foggiest idea what they were talking about. I had specifically campaigned on crime in the streets, commies on campuses, and sin in general. I had no recourse but a "Hmmmmmm," nod and question.

"Hmmmmmm," I would say. "What do *you* think we should do?" It usually works. They give their solution and I "Hmmmmmm" some more and nod again. Sometimes, for good measure, I would throw in "I'll be darned." If you are patient enough, sooner or later someone will ask you about something you really know. Then filibuster. It takes either tenacity or downright rudeness for someone to get you to change the subject.

What shocked me, though, was that they actually believed I understood all of these different subject areas. Doctors asking questions about legislation affecting them—lawyers, CPAs, businessmen, all the same. I was the same person on November 4 that I had been on November 3. The only difference was that I had a title. I was now a bona fide senator.

No matter what they tell you, or what you may want to believe, legislators are actually human. The successful politician, however, is usually the one capable of creating the impression that he is all-knowing and on top of the matter. Actually, there is no magic, no subliminal infusion of knowledge, no anointing by the gods, no special gift of knowledge from above that is awarded to the gladiator emerging victorious. Though worshiped by many in politics, Demos (mythical god of the majority) has yet to make a single legislator any brighter through the baptism of the electoral process.

The problem with this notion of "instant smart" is that before long, some elected officials begin to believe it themselves. It has been my experience that there is nothing more dangerous on God's green earth than a well-meaning legislator trying to solve all social problems.

There is no magic in a simple majority. The title that comes with the job tends to impress most Americans, but outside of a little more social acceptance, convivial admiration from relatives and friends, and better seating in fancy restaurants, the title "senator," "congressman" or "assemblyman" confers not one share of added brainpower.

4

Gangrene and the Board of Education

To ERR is human and legislators are most human. The only difference is that when we err it is often on network TV.

Television and the movies have given legislators an erroneous image. Cast in the role of villains, we are usually portrayed as planning, scheming demons of iniquity. When, on the other hand, we are projected as wise and reasoned community leaders, our every endeavor is interpreted as noble and well conceived. In either case, we are portrayed as knowing what we are doing. Whether it be good or bad, we are cast as mentally organized.

Sometimes nothing could be further from the truth; reams of laws have come into existence by fumbling, stumbling, and accident. Poorly conceived and clumsily drafted laws are not the exception to the rule. It's easily proved. Every year legislation is introduced to "clean up" last year's boo-boo. Something unforeseen is constantly cropping up—something that requires a new law to be passed. Legislators can be kept busy for the next fifty years correcting and recorrecting old mistakes, or in legislative language, "bringing the laws up to date."

A number of years ago, several legislators got the bright idea of breaking up the Los Angeles school system into smaller units. The Los Angeles City School System is larger than roughly half of the state departments of education across America. It is a glowing symbol of educational bureaucracy,

19

an educational edifice of mediocrity managed by a conglomerate of educators who have master's degrees in implementing the Peter principle.

Los Angeles schools have excelled in the production of functional illiterates. Nowhere else, outside of New York, have so many diplomas been given to so many students who have so deserved them less. Los Angeles schools have made the "six Rs" a household word—remedial reading, remedial riting, and remedial rithmetic. Nowhere else. is this more evident than in the n   inal areas of Los Angeles.

It was no surprise that several assemblymen from the black area of Los Angeles were eager to break up the Los Angeles school system. The hope was that smaller districts would create more parental control over curriculum and student activity. The bill was cointroduced by several liberal members of the black community, myself, and an outspoken conservative. What appeared to be an unorthodox assortment of authors was in reality two groups committed to the same end, but for different reasons. I supported the bill because I believed in a smaller school system and more parental control. My black colleagues viewed it as a means by which they (the black liberals) could have greater political power over local education. The Los Angeles school system is dominated by white liberals, and the black liberals saw this as a vehicle to accomplish their goal of seizing part of the educational cake.

The bill was introduced, accompanied by press releases. We all sat back and waited for the inevitable reactions. They were not long in coming. The Los Angeles Board of Education immediately defended its honor, but, in a surprise move, offered to meet with us, the members of the state legislature, to resolve our differences. "Meet and resolve differences" translated means let's get together so we can talk you out of what you have in mind, or let's get together so we can so confuse the issue that no action is taken. We accepted. We had no choice. The meeting was scheduled in the county building where the Los Angeles supervisors meet. The hearing room was a sizable auditorium with a slightly elevated stage.

The supervisors had luxurious accommodations. When in session, they and their staff sat around an immense half-curved table complete with microphones. Instead of the supervisors, the school-board members sat on one side; and we legislators, who authored the bill, sat on the other. The grand confrontation was about to begin.

The meeting was very well attended, especially by the media. All of the local TV stations were there, along with the local press and numerous representatives from radio. Microphones and TV cameras covered the speakers' podium.

We, the legislators, had met briefly to discuss strategy. After a few intelligent remarks like, "Hey, what are we going to do today?" we decided to follow one colleague's advice— "Let's play it by ear." We all agreed that this was the proper course. "Play it by ear" usually means wait for an opening, hope the other side blunders, then pounce.

The press wanted one of us to make opening remarks. We all agreed that a particular black member of our group was the perfect choice. He was big and had a beautiful deep, resonant voice. In fact, his voice was so deep, he made singers of "Old Man River" sound like tenors. At the appointed hour, the blinding TV lights came on, the cameras started to roll, and the great educational confrontation between Sacramento and Los Angeles began.

Our spokesman looked down to his notes, raised his head dramatically, paused, then spoke. The assemblyman's voice started quietly then rose perceptibly and dramatically as he immersed himself in his subject matter. What was at stake? Children's education! What else! Why were we here? To save the children, of course! What was the problem? Inferior quality of education, no doubt! His deep voice grew louder and louder. The rafters were vibrating with the rich, resonant tones. The heat of the bright lights only accented the emotion of the moment. Soon the central theme of his remarks became evident. There was "a gaping education wound" within the Los Angeles school system—"a gaping wound" that needed to be healed.

It was a good theme, and the assemblyman was making the most of it. His voice was strong and quaking with emotion as he came to the close. Sweat trickled down his black face. Righteous indignation was emblazoned on his countenance and justice poured from his very soul—"Ladies and gentlemen, members of the school board, we must close and heal this wound." He paused dramatically. The audience was hushed. He looked down to his notes, paused once more, then finished. "We must heal this great wound before it turns into gonorrhea! . . . no, no . . . gangrene! I meant, gangrene!"

Then, while the cameramen, radio reporters, and members of the audience were collapsing in the aisles with laughter, the assemblyman, with a silly, embarrassed grin stretching from ear to ear, pointed to his notes and remarked, "By gosh, that's what I wrote—gonorrhea!"

Needless to say, we never recovered our dignity. The rest of the day was spent looking into the Mona Lisa faces of the smiling members of the Los Angeles Board of Education. Any dignity we had was demolished. Later on, the bill died quietly on the floor of the assembly.

5

Legislators: A Most Pleasant Lot

LEGISLATORS ARE the most pleasant group of men one could ever care to meet. They are affable, glib, fun-loving, joke-telling, quick to laugh, friendly, and generally courteous. They are usually good mixers and appear comfortable and relaxed in most gatherings, possessing an uncanny ability to sense the mood and temperament of those with whom they are mixing. Astute is perhaps the word that best describes success-ful politicos. They are professional at being pleasant and charming.

It stands to reason that most of them are pleasant, otherwise they would be "unelectable, unselectable, and unpaid." Can you imagine a cantankerous introvert being elected or, for that matter, even wanting to be a politician? Would a humorless, unfriendly candidate succeed? Hardly! People like their rep-resentatives to be "nice guys," and that is what they have elected, nice guys.

Socially, I can't think of a more charming group to be around. If sociability were the sole criterion for choosing comradeship, politicians would have to rank number one. Conversationally, they can usually discuss a wide variety of subjects. They are masterful at disagreeing without being unpleasant. It is part of the profession. Philosophically, it is a different story.

Politicos are seasoned salesmen. The products they sell are themselves, and good product-packaging requires a pleasant exterior.

There are few lazy incumbents. You can call legislators every name in the book, but lazy shouldn't be one of them. To remain elected, an incumbent must stay on his toes, because there is always some dastardly rogue trying to woo his constituency away from him.

Once a United States senator from California received a panic call from his aide.

"Senator, you must come home at once. They are telling lies about you in Los Angeles!"

"I'm coming home at once," the senator responded. "My flight arrives in San Francisco this afternoon!"

"But, senator," the aide replied, "they are telling lies about you in Los Angeles."

"I know," replied the senator, "but they are telling the truth about me in San Francisco!"

Rarely does a person achieve any elected office by accident. The campaign trail is a trying test of a man's ability to absorb punishment, long stressful hours, pressure, conflict, and risks. All too often, able opponents scare the heebie-jeebies out of him. The elective process is a fire that tests a man's political steel.

It can be quite disconcerting successfully to seek a legislative position and then serve with an "enemy" politician whom you find to be Mr. Charm himself.

How delightfully simple it would be if all of my political opposition were rotters, cads, and unsavory characters, and conveniently looked the part. How much easier it would be to discredit their specious arguments if they had horns and fangs. It is much easier to dislike a man who kicks dogs, cusses in front of ladies, scowls incessantly, and needs industrial-strength Right Guard.

How much easier it would be to convince the politically uninformed of the logic of my position if only those who opposed my ideas were cads and curs. How convenient if my opposition mouthed indifference to the plight of orphans, widows, and the disabled, and publicly showed their callousness. It would be so much easier for voters to appreciate my position.

If only my philosophical opposition would wear black uniforms with shiny black boots and jackets with "bad guy" printed on the front and back. How much simpler it would be for me to point them out to one and all as ill equipped to deal with sensitive human problems.

Alas, it is not so. Some of my most vocal political opponents are charming, articulate, and astute. They like dogs, love their children, and if they beat their wives, I am unaware of it. They dress and act conservatively, and are usually unabashedly pleasant. They have the audacity to say *they* are for improving the plight of orphans, widows, and the disabled, and that I am the villain!

In most cases, the differences between politicos are in that gray matter that resides between the ears—differences that cannot be seen, but only perceived.

The basic premises which determine a politician's view of life, his philosophy, are what really count. These are not as discernible as a suit of clothes or a winning smile. It is the ideas to which a legislator adheres that have consequences, not the personality projected to the voting public.

There are exceptions to every rule, and politics is no different. Occasionally, we get a legislator who is humorless and looks like an unmade bed—and on rare occasions we find a fat one who will smoke cigars in public.

Once there was a humorless legislator who looked upon smiling as a bourgeois trait, unbecoming to a conscientious proletarian socialist.

He would slink up and down the halls with a hound-dog look, muttering Chicken Littleisms under his breath. He suffered. Oh, how he suffered! He agonized for everybody except big business and the FBI. Anyone else was exploited and, therefore, his personal cross to bear. Life was tragedy, and the oppressed, the downtrodden, the exploited masses were his constituency. He gave the distinct impression that he was the only *real* protector in the legislature because only *he* visibly suffered for The Cause.

Legislators are usually sharp dressers, and sackcloth and ashes aren't in style. Ties and coats are expected to be worn on the floors of the assembly and the senate. My colleague was in a quandary. How does one dressed in a suit "identify" with the suffering masses? How does one establish a "meaningful dialogue" with oppressed minorities while wearing the uniform (suit, tie, shoes, vest) of the enemy? How can one be in tune with nonconformity unless one wears the uniform of the nonconformists? (Faded blue jeans, blue shirt, sandals or barefoot, handcrafted leather belt, beads, pierced earring in left ear, uncombed hair—preferably long—and a roach clip partially exposed.)

My proletarian colleague had a problem, how to, but not to. He resolved it to his semisatisfaction by wearing regular clothes in a contemptuous fashion—necktie partly tied and loose at the neck, shirt partially buttoned and no T-shirt underneath so belly-button hair could occasionally be exposed. He accomplished the impossible; he wrinkled polyester. His jackets always looked as though the wrinkles were ironed in intentionally. He allowed his hair to grow and then frizzed it into an Afro. His appearance on the floor of the senate was always a memorable occasion. Planned chaos. An obvious proletarian in bourgeois garb.

Since I was the enemy, he always wore his worst scowl in my presence. Whenever I saw him before he spotted me, I gave him the treatment. Since he liked to suffer, I tried to help him as much as I could. No matter how depressed I felt at the time, I suddenly transformed myself into Sir Bubbly, Mr. Happiness and Jovial Jack. I would walk past him vigorously with a smile plastered across my face, my voice bubbling with glad tidings. "Hi, pal! Great day, isn't it?"

It never failed. It drove him bananas. Gloom would settle over him like a cloud of nuclear dust. To him it was obvious that my joy could only mean that some poor soul or group or class had been exploited.

The constant pressure of the legislature became too much for him and he left the hallowed halls for other pursuits, carrying with him the weight of the world and an armful of wrinkled polyester suits. I'll miss him. At least he was a distinctive individual.

Legislators are a pleasant lot, but don't equate being a "good guy" with being a good legislator.

Which is preferable, an unpleasant, ornery legislator who protects your liberties, or a Smiling Jack who wants to rule you from cradle to coffin? The answer, I hope, is obvious.

6

What's A Seat Worth?

WHAT IS A SEAT in the legislature worth?

Not too long ago a special election was held for a vacated seat in the California State Senate. By the time the dust had settled, over $400,000 was spent to elect a new man to the office.

People asked, "Why was so much money spent for a job that pays only $21,000?" Answer: Because of what the job represents. A state legislator may vote on expenditures exceeding eighteen billion dollars, and often a single vote can be very important.

Eighteen billion dollars. That's a lot of money. I could give you a few staggering examples of how much a billion is, but just try to count dollars (one dollar, two dollars, etc.) as fast as you can. Go ahead, try it. If your voice and lungs could hold out, in about an hour you would be up to 9,800 dollars. In a twenty-four-hour day you would be up to 135,200; in a week, 946,400; and in a month, 4,056,000. A year would take you to a little over forty-eight million. In other words, yakking away as fast as you can, you haven't even dented a billion in a whole year. In fact, if you started counting on your first birthday, you couldn't count to eighteen billion if you lived to be 360 years old.

If that doesn't stagger you, nothing will. Yet, a billion dollars is how much the California legislature spends in less than one month and the feds do it in a single day. When a legislative body taxes and dispenses enormous amounts of capital, you can bet your bottom dollar that those who want their share are going to make a beeline to the hallowed halls of the legislature and that the legislators are going to receive a great deal of attention from both the GOTS and the WANTS.

Those who have a vested interest in maintaining the power of the legislature play an inordinate role in perpetuating their favorites in office or electing "their kind of men."

"Their kind of men" usually means the kind that can be counted upon to vote the "right" way on bills relating to the industry.

Let me offer an example of a group that has a great deal to gain from the "right" decisions by the legislature.

The CTA (California Teachers Association) represents approximately 200,000 teachers in California. Most teachers belong to this group. The teaching profession is heavily influenced by the actions of the legislature. Their tenure, sabbatical leaves, vacations, sick pay, retirement, salaries, and a host of privileges are directly influenced by the actions of the legislature.

Quite a number of years ago the teachers employed a little elementary arithmetic and discovered that it is a lot easier dealing with a handful of legislators than having to influence each school board in the state. In fact, all that need be done is to control the committees that hear education bills. In the senate, eight of the eleven members of the education committee receive substantial contributions from the California Teachers Association.

Some folks think that lobby money comes into play only after a candidate has been elected. The prevailing assumption is that every new legislator arriving in Sacramento is a political maiden waiting to be deflowered by some unscrupulous lobbyists.

Actually, pressure groups are seldom attracted to political Pollyannas. Most successful pressure groups are active in the primary campaigns, trying to get "their kind of statesman" nominated. One may be sure they will have checked out the candidate's "feelings" on certain matters.

For a flight into fancy, imagine the representatives of the California Teachers Association, the extremely powerful and well-heeled teachers' union, interviewing a candidate in the following manner:

CTA: Do you believe that teachers are underpaid?

CANDIDATE: Teachers are overpaid, by and large. If anything, some teachers' salaries should be cut while others should be raised. I believe in a merit system.

CTA: Hmm! How do you view our tenure laws?

CANDIDATE: I believe they should be abolished. Too many incompetent teachers hide behind tenure and should be dismissed.

CTA: Mercy! Do you believe in collective bargaining for teachers and the right of teachers to strike?

CANDIDATE: I do not! I believe the educators have a captive monopoly on education and secure jobs that preempt those rights. Any teacher who strikes should be fired!

CTA: Golly jeepers! Thank you, sir, for your frank opinions. We certainly respect your right to your views, and because we believe that the legislature should be a forum for all kinds of opinions, we are going to contribute heartily to your campaign.

Quite a fairy tale, isn't it?

If you know anyone who believes that the CTA hands out campaign contributions under the above circumstances, then protect him. It won't be long before somebody sells him that bridge that stretches from Oakland to San Francisco.

When the day arrives that the CTA or a union gives money to its opposition, then Bambi will rule the forest, Alice will have returned from Wonderland, children will refuse free passes to Disneyland, and lawyers will turn down cases because of ethical considerations.

Candidates who run for political office are screened, reviewed, and, if there is a possibility of their being successful, financially helped by special-interest groups.

This brings up a very important point. Most candidates usually have a certain philosophical perspective *before* they are elected, and it is often because of their "reliability" that special-interest groups such as the State Employees Association and the teachers unions support them.

The public-employee unions and other special interests then become the candidate's constituency. For all practical purposes they are willing to cast green bread upon the political waters. Money is needed to get elected and then reelected. Printers are swell guys and so are typesetters and copywriters and photographers, but each has definite mandrake capabilities. To prove my point, just ask one voluntarily to give of his time and effort to compose a campaign brochure. Watch him vanish into thin air.

Campaigns are costly and all of the gobbledygook about broad citizen participation is usually restricted to voting. Less than one percent of all registered voters contribute directly to political campaigns. People are willing to part with their opinions but not with their money. Those who do contribute gain the ear of the candidate. There are those who contribute because they like to support men who reflect their own political principles and who ask nothing but that the candidate stay faithful to his beliefs. These are usually the politically active party faithful.

Some people contribute because they are familiar with the candidate and want someone elected whom they know. I call these volunteer contributors. They are important, and if a candidate receives the bulk of his contributions from these sources, he has a greater degree of independence. But in many cases, this constituency is the minority. Soliciting this kind of contribution takes time and usually these contributions are small by comparison. The CTA drops $10,000 at a time. Most hometown contributors who donate $25 feel like philanthropists.

It's a rare day someone calls a candidate and says, "Charlie, I hear you are running for office. My $1,000 check is in the mail and if it's not enough, I'll send more.''

If any candidate or officeholder says that he received the bulk of his contributions in unsolicited donations, don't leave your wallet unattended. Chances are, the truth is not his constant companion. Contributions rarely come without effort. Even churches have to solicit funds every Sunday. Ushers systematically walk up the aisles with empty receptacles waiting to be filled. If the Lord's churches have to ask, no one else is immune from passing the plate, least of all, politicians.

Most solons like being in the legislature, so the contributor who puts the biggest hunk of folding money into the platter is the one who gets to sit in the first political pew.

It would not be fair if I didn't mention another kind of lobbyist who rattles around the legislative halls. They are not called lobbyists. But for all intents and purposes, that is what they are. These are the "representatives" of the many government agencies and bureaus that have so much to gain or lose by legislative action. These stalwarts of verbal evasion are supposed authorities who are sent forth to advise the legislature on matters affecting their departments.

Bureaucrats assigned to represent the different departments before the legislative committees are the most masterful practitioners of the art of omission. With unbounded authority they speak longer than most, and say less more eloquently than any other group of witnesses.

Everyone has heard of the professional lobbyists, those who are employed by industry, labor, "consumer" groups, et al., but rarely does one think of a governmental department as having lobbyists who come before committees. Nonetheless, they do exist and they do lobby for a particular point of view—that of their respective departments.

If a bill causes displeasure, one can count on the department's representative to be present and accounted for when the committee is called to order. Even if that department has no "official position" one can rest assured that it will get its two cents in one way or another. Many a governor has found that the administration he supposedly controls often sabotages his own favorite legislation. There are few politicians equal to an upper-level civil servant in the art of guile, and no greased pig at the county fair can match a civil-service public-relations man who doesn't want to answer a direct question.

After many years, it must become habit-forming. I know a representative for the State Department of Education who doesn't have *yes* or *no* in his vocabulary.

One must remember that these department representatives are paid to be professional noncommittors. All of them are chock-full of statistics, dates, surveys, and conference reports—miniunivacs in unobtrusive suits, ready to spout irrelevant information whenever needed to confuse inquiring legislators.

It's a fact: one better know the answer before the question is asked, if one wants the straight dope from a bureaucrat. Also, the departmental expert must be convinced that the legislator can find out the answer before he will respond accurately.

Legislators can be a threat to the bureaucracy, so we are always a potential problem to the sanctimonious civil servant. One may be assured that the representative assigned to feed the legislators whatever they "need" to know will be the best silver-tongued smoothy the department has to offer.

Lobbying is only for those with the toughest hide, the smoothest smile, and the calm befitting a saint. Ruffled feathers are a no-no; anger is not cool. Those who can't handle the action soon retire.

A number of years ago a new lobbyist for the foreign-language teachers association asked for an appointment so that he could lobby me on a bill dear to the hearts of all foreign-language teachers. The bill would have required study of foreign languages in the elementary grades—a real plum for all of the unemployed foreign-language teachers.

He was a pleasant chap. I assumed a relaxed pose and we had a delightful discussion about education in general and the importance of learning for the little tots. The bill he was lobbying for proposed expanding, as he stated, "the opportunities to enrich a child's learning experience." I asked him why he thought a child needed to study Spanish, French, or German in the fifth grade. What was the value to the child?

"Senator," he replied, "language is a meaningful experience. Someday that child may find himself in a foreign land and he would be capable of communicating with people of other countries, thereby enriching his life and bringing greater understanding among people of the world." He smiled, reclined in his chair peacefully. I'm sure he thought he had given me a beautiful thought for the day. He was ill prepared for my response.

"Horse pucky," I replied. I leaned forward and glared at him from over my desk. "Our colleges are graduating boatloads of teachers who have majored in foreign languages and they can't find jobs. Your job is to get legislation passed which mandates expanded foreign-language programs so that more foreign-language teachers can be hired!" He sat there with his mouth agape, stunned. Obviously, nobody had questioned his pitch before now.

I continued. "Listen, we're barely teaching kids to read English. Few can properly structure a sentence by fifth grade, and now you want to cram a foreign language down their throats—a language that ninety-five percent will forget by the time they reach the age of fifteen. Most of them will be lucky to remember what 'adios' means." I was purposely rough on him. He was new and I wanted to see how he would react.

"Boy, you're tough!" he replied.

"Well," I shot back, "it's true, isn't it?"

"Well, er, ah, uh," he stammered. He was too honest to say I was wrong and too chicken to say yes. He mumbled a lot and beat a hasty retreat from my office. Needless to say, he didn't last long as a lobbyist. I ran into him a few years after, and he was comfortably ensconced in a job that did not require legislative contact. He seemed much happier.

An effective representative for those who constantly seek

governmental handouts from the taxpayer goody-wagon must have a passel of defensive clichés ready for all occasions and the ability to slip a verbal punch with the agility of a trained boxer.

A proper and accepted response to my verbal blast would have been to use the "wide-eyed and wounded" technique. First, open the eyes as wide as possible and hold them open for at least five to ten seconds. Then draw back, if seated, or step back if standing, and stagger imperceptibly to create the impression of being mortally wounded. "Senator! How *can* you say that! We are just interested in the well-being of the children. Language is an important part of the learning experience and foreign-language teachers spend years learning how to master communication. Why, if nations could speak to each other we could possibly stop wars. . ."

See what I mean? A real pro would have feigned a mortal wound and then bled all over me. I would have been an isolationist for opposing his bill, a child-hater, and, of course, a warmonger.

An effective legislative advocate learns to live the role and as the famous dramatist Chayefsky stated, "If you are going to play the part of an apple, *be* an apple." If you are going to be a legislative advocate, *believe* in that turkey legislation and dare any opponent to doubt the efficacy of your gobbler.

Lobbyists are here to stay—that is, as long as the people keep turning over their hard-earned money for legislators to dole out to whom they see fit.

Lobbyists and legislators—like Bonnie and Clyde.

7

Read The Bills!

IN THE INTEREST of relieving human suffering, I feel obliged to warn the reader in advance about the subject matter of this chapter. It is about the mechanics of the actual lawmaking process.

It has been noted that those who like sausages should not watch them being made. Former Governor Reagan remarked on one occasion that the same rule applies to the making of laws.

Forewarned, we continue.

It was a dull day on the floor of the senate. Most of the legislation being heard was "noncontroversial." That means bills with little media interest or minimal constituent concern.

Legislator after legislator explained his bill and took questions. Most bills were cruising through the senate with little, if any, debate. The author would answer a question or two and then ask for an aye vote. The whole process took five minutes, at most.

One bill caught the attention of one of my colleagues, and he stood to ask the author the intent of certain language. I reached up and pulled the folder that contained the bills and looked at the one under consideration. It was a typical legislative bowser. In other words, a dog. Every desk has a microphone attached to a rocker arm. I raised mine, signifying to the presiding officer that I wanted to speak on the bill. I asked a question or two and satisfied myself that a no vote was in order.

As I sat down, another colleague was raising his mike. He has definite mannerisms which telegraph his future actions. Whenever he plans to speak against a bill, he raises himself to his feet in a most deliberate manner, then ever so slowly turns to face the body and delivers his negative oration. He was now about halfway through his turn when the legislator who sits next to him loudly whispered, "King, you voted for that bill in committee." "I know," he responded quietly, "but I just read the bill."

Uncommon? Not at all. Legislators usually do not read all of the legislation they vote on. In fact, it's a rare legislative bird who even reads most of the bills. In the many years I've served in the legislature I know of only one man who might have reviewed all the legislation on which he voted. He carried a little green ruler in his pocket and systematically read bills using that green ruler as a guide.

His conscientiousness was rewarded with the respect of his colleagues and defeat at the polls. Reading the bills is not a prerequisite for getting elected.

One of the shocks that Californians rarely recover from is watching their legislators in action. People have a subconscious image of how the legislators operate on the floor and when they have a firsthand opportunity to observe their leaders, the inner doubts begin. Most people believe that the legislative process is serious business.

Laws restrict, deny, tax, regulate, and can bring the police power of the state down around one's head if he fails to observe those laws. Americans are law-abiding, and they hope that the legislature constructs laws seriously and deliberately. All of this implies dignity and attentiveness on the part of their solons. It's quite a letdown to observe, during the explanation of a bill, groups of legislators talking and laughing with each other, seemingly oblivious to the debate; some members reading correspondence, others the newspaper, while two legislators debate the bill. It takes getting used to.

Legislators consistently vote on legislation without understanding what is in it, especially when the final vote is taken.

Every legislator has his own system for judging how he will vote, but reading the bill usually isn't part of the procedure, and listening to debate on the bill's merits certainly isn't either.

I am not implying that legislators don't read the bills; some of them do. Usually an author will read his own bill because it can be quite embarrassing to have a colleague point out something in it that the author hasn't read. That is not an uncommon occurrence.

A number of years ago, the author of one bill rose to present the salient facts of his legislation to the assembled body. His presentation was of moderate length as he explained the reason for the bill's adoption.

Across the room a microphone was raised and one of the more eloquent members of the assembly rose to address himself to the bill. "Mr. Speaker and gentlemen of the assembly: We have here before us a bill that is poor legislation at best, a disaster to the state at worst. Why, if this becomes law . . ." The eloquent orator went on and on about the inadequacies of the bill, the damage to the state and nation that would be caused if it became law; motherhood, apple pie, and baseball were at stake. The bill was a calamity, an affront to the legislative process. A turkey.

Caught up in the enthusiasm of his attack, the eloquent orator was oblivious to the legislator who sits at the desk right next to his. As unobtrusively as he could, his seatmate was trying to get the attention of his vocal colleague by tugging at his pant leg. "Psst, Charlie, psst." (Pull, tug.) "Psst, Charlie." The "pssts" became louder and the tugs more pronounced. Everybody heard the "pssts," but the loquacious assemblyman was not to be constrained by the now violent pulling at his pant leg. Finally, after a tug that almost depanted him, the vocal legislator stopped momentarily. Covering the microphone with one hand, the orator leaned over and whispered, "What in the heck do you want? Can't you see I'm in the middle of a debate?"

His seatmate replied, "Take a look at the cover of the bill, bigmouth. You're a cosponsor!"

Without batting an eyelash, our articulate assemblyman returned to the task at hand. "Gentlemen of the assembly, I have just presented all of the specious arguments that have been used against this fine piece of legislation. I thought it only fair to present the opposition's views first before I display this outstanding bill's merits for your consideration." Then, in glowing terms, the legislator talked an equal amount of time on the glories of the bill.

People make a lot of assumptions about their representatives. One of the biggest is that legislators read the bills.

In the case of the loquacious assemblyman, he hadn't even read the bill's cover page. If he had, he would have seen that his name was on it. It is not unheard of to see legislators vote or argue against bills that they have coauthored. Don't be shocked by the fact that legislators don't read every bill. It would be more shocking if they did. Demands upon a legislator are so heavy that the reading of bills is usually delegated to staff or to a committee consultant. Only key bills receive the legislator's full attention. Most bills that pass are seldom read by even a majority of the legislators who vote on them.

Each bill has a brief analysis and for the most part, that suffices. Each caucus staff prepares a summary of the bill and in many cases that isn't read either.

Once one understands what the public expects of its legislators, it is no surprise that reading the legislation is of secondary importance to many of them.

Anyone who has ever read a bill can understand why the legislators hire staff to explain, or as we say, analyze and research, the legislation. Every bill either adds something to or changes the existing language of present laws, which means that to understand the proposed new law one should understand the old one. The bill has italicized print to indicate newly proposed language and a line through the deleted portions. It is not too difficult to understand the first bill, but once the bill is changed in any way (amended), then, take my word for it, it gets sticky to follow, because all the language that had a line through it is gone—in the newly printed, amended bill.

If the bill has been amended several times, and usually all substantive bills are, then one has to refer back to the previously amended bill to see what is going on. I could make this a lot more complicated, but I think you get the idea.

Properly to understand most bills, the code sections have to be researched to see what is being changed. Some bills are hundreds of pages long, complicated monstrosities amending and repealing previous code sections. We don't just read the original bill. Every time a bill has a major amendment, it has to be reread. I have seen bills start out in one direction and, over the jagged course of amendments, be heading 180 degrees in another direction a few weeks later. There are many steps along the way that should demand the constant attention of a legislator. It is a superhuman task to be aware of every bill and, whether we like to admit it or not, legislators are not superhuman.

More often than not, a legislator sees a particular bill for the first time when he sits down in his chair in the committee room. He usually turns to the analysis of the bill and reads it quickly before someone moves the bill out with a "do pass." If no opposition is expressed, the bill usually goes sliding out. The prevailing rule of thumb nowadays is, when in doubt, vote aye.

Unless a bill is controversial, it usually isn't read word for word by the legislators, even in committee. Because of the volume of bills, the legislature is broken down into committees. The object is to analyze the legislation in detail. That doesn't happen often. Why? Because of the time problem.

The committee may have twenty or more bills on the agenda and its task is to "hear" these bills within a three-hour time frame. That means if every bill is heard, the average time given each bill would be nine minutes. It obviously doesn't work that way. Some receive more time and some zip through.

The bigger the load on the agenda, the more quickly they slide through. Once in a while a bill is defeated, but not often.

The committee staff analyzes the bills, taking each one and, as concisely as it can, trying to explain in writing what it does. These analyses are placed in a book for each legislator and presented to him when he comes to the committee room.

Controversial bills receive more attention and on occasion long hearings are given to major bills, but more legislation sails through than not.

Every bill has the force of police power behind it. Every bill changes the method of how laws are enforced. While the public takes notice of the big bills, I suspect that it is actually the cumulative impact of hundreds of "noncontroversial" rules and regulations that are strangling this state and nation.

Each legislator sits on only a few committees. The majority of the bills with which he comes into contact he will see on the floor of the senate or assembly for the first time.

Some bills are deemed so noncontroversial that we even have reserved for them a special place in the legislative voting process that we call the Consent Calendar. These bills are so noncontroversial that to save time, the legislature votes on all of them at once. On one occasion late in the session, when things were all jammed up, we had a great number of bills on the Consent Calendar. In one fell swoop we voted on twenty-five bills at one time.

Do you believe that a legislator drafts his own bills? If you said yes, then you're wrong again. The legislature has a flock of full-time lawyers to counsel legislators and draft ninety-nine percent of all the bills. This Legislative Counsel, as it is called in California, consists of sixty lawyers at a yearly cost of $4,588,367 to the state. When a legislator wishes to draft a bill, he calls in a lawyer and explains what he wants his bill to do. The lawyer from Legislative Counsel then goes back to his private office and drafts the bill for the legislator.

It is not unusual to see a legislator before a committee presenting what he thinks is his idea, only to find that there has been a lack of communication between the legislator and legislative counselor who drafted the bill. It gets a wee bit embarrassing to present what one thinks the bill does only to find that the consultant to the committee thinks it does something else. Sometimes the author doesn't even read his *own* bill until he is before the committee to which the bill has been assigned. Sometimes he doesn't even *see* the committee on his own legislation.

Some legislators authorize a lobbyist or an administrative assistant to present their bills before committee. The first time he sees his own bill may be when he presents it to the full body of the senate or the assembly. It gets a bit sticky when an author is questioned on his own legislation and he doesn't have the answers.

About this time you should be asking yourself, well, if they don't read the bills, how do legislators make up their minds on how to vote?

Good question. (That is, if you asked it.) The volume of legislation and lack of time force members to develop certain techniques. Some slavishly follow the recommendations of labor organizations. The unions say no, so no it is. If the education lobby doesn't like it, then no, no, a thousand times no. A sizable number of legislators have a deep philosophical commitment to government regulation and if the administration wants it, then it is okay by them.

Some check with other legislators who think as they do. If one's philosophical friend serves on the Committee on Insurance and Financial Institutions and votes aye, then one may be inclined to vote aye also.

The political parties at times take caucus positions and some solons would rather die than break ranks with the party.

Some identify with different popular movements and support all legislation heading in their direction. Only a few try to guess what would please the majority of their constituents.

A number of years ago there was a very colorful and dynamic senator who had captured the imagination and loyalty of the rank and file on a statewide basis. He was constantly asked to speak before politically active groups. His voting record was used by the philosophically faithful as a standard by which to evaluate other senators. Senator Super had his philosophy screwed on tightly, and verbally demonstrated his intellectual prowess with consistent regularity.

Some legislators, finding it philosophically comfortable, piggybacked the vote of Senator Super. "I voted on that issue with Senator Super" could often evoke applause amongst the true believers.

One solon found it a particularly comforting habit. Senator Super's district was close to his own and his popularity overlapped the district lines.

Senator Ditto was also a nervous sort. Whenever he received letters on both sides of an issue, his political sweat glands became overactive. Not knowing exactly what to do, since his own philosophical drives were weak, he eagerly awaited the vote of Senator Super. He never, I believe, ever understood the reasons for these particular votes. His own philosophy was simple: get reelected. So, slavishly, he would vote according to the voting pattern of Senator Super.

One day Senator Super voted for a bill that was inconsistent with his basic outlook. In a weak moment he had committed to vote for this particular bill and was fulfilling his commitment.

Several of the legislators descended upon their newly errant comrade. "Why in heaven's name did you vote for that piece of junk?" they demanded.

Whereupon Senator Super admitted, "Ah, in a weak moment I got conned into supporting it and I've given my word." Because the senator was a very ethical individual, his colleagues found it difficult to fault the man for keeping his commitment. To be sure, the legislator was extremely upset over having to give an affirmative vote to this particular measure, but he felt that his honor was at stake. Obviously, Senator Ditto had voted affirmatively also.

Fortunately, the bill didn't have the required number of

votes for passage and a "call" was put on this particular measure. A call can occur when the final vote has not been counted and the author of the bill is allowed to try to find any absent senators to see if they could be committed to vote.

Seizing upon this lull in the proceedings, Senator Super's disappointed colleagues approached him and said, "Hey, buddy, you've only committed to vote for the bill once, which you've done. But does that necessarily mean that you have to continue to commit to it?"

One could almost see a bulb light over his head. "You're right," he said. He threw up his microphone and when recognized by the chair, he said, "Mr. President, I choose to switch my aye vote to nay."

With a confused look, Senator Ditto threw up his microphone and changed his vote from aye to nay.

The author of the bill made a beeline for Senator Super. "You gave me your word," he said, "that you would vote affirmatively on this particular bill. What kind of guy are you, backing out on your word?"

The legislator responded, "Well, I've already voted for your bill once, and I have a difficult time supporting this kind of measure. I met my commitment by voting for your bill once."

The other legislator responded, "That is a real chicken way out of holding your promise."

Senator Super, seeing that he had done nothing more than seize upon momentary opportunity, raised his microphone and wearily said, "Mr. President, how am I recorded?"

The secretary said, "You are recorded as voting nay."

The legislator then said, "Nay to aye."

By this time the copycat senator was going nuts. He had changed his vote twice, but true to form, he raised his microphone and for the third time correspondingly changed his vote.

There are many other reasons why a legislator votes aye or nay. Sometimes it is sweet revenge—a fellow colleague kills one of a legislator's favorite bills or incurs his wrath by waging an articulate debate against it. Some wait for the opportunity to stick it to him. There is an old expression, "Don't get mad— get even."

Sometimes it is a payoff vote for a favor done. An unspoken favor, because the laws supposedly are there to stop legislative logrolling (which means you roll my log and I'll roll yours, or you vote for my turkey and I'll bring you a case of cranberries).

Sometimes it is raw pressure. Even though one may think it is not a good piece of legislation, some pressure group will make life miserable for those who vote against it or make reelection easier for those who see the "logic" of the affirmative case. I call this "power logic." There is a corny old joke about two men playing poker. One called and asked, "What you got?"

The man replied, "Four aces. What you got?"

The first said, "A pair of deuces and a knife!"

Whereupon the second replied, "You win again. I have never seen such a run of luck!"

Power logic at its best.

I have my own criteria. If a bill misuses the regulatory power of government or expands programs or costs more money, I vote no. That eliminates one heck of a lot of bills in a big hurry. There are a number of legislators who are philosophically 180 degrees from me and whenever I see a bill with their names as authors, I make a beeline for the bill in question. I am sure they do the same to my bills.

I hope you will have noticed that I haven't mentioned logic and reason as factors in how legislators vote. In the many years I have served in the state legislature, no one has ever approached me and stated, "Bill, your premises are inaccurate," or, for my intellectual friends, "I would like to discuss the fallacy of your epistemological presuppositions." Not once in ten years has this happened. The legislature is not a body of intellectuals contemplating the origin of man's being or the system of government best adapted to the nature of human character, but, rather, a body of men reacting to what they deem the most successful way to be reelected.

It is imagined to be a reflective body, but it is not—nor can it ever be. Not as long as men are expected to play gods and those elected believe they can. The system creates problems, and with a full-time state legislature, those elected are voting aye on more and more bills and knowing less and less about them.

8

200 Secrets

POLITICS IS no place for the thin-skinned. Like fruit in a supermarket, the thin-skinned produce soon bruises and rots, and is no longer marketable. A politician must have the hide of a rhinoceros to last on the shelf of politics. Survival within the framework of political life demands it.

Few professions bring one into contact with so many different varieties of humanoids. One thing is certain, the Lord surely believed in diversity. He never made any two of us alike.

Not surprisingly, that diversity extends to the realm of political opinion. Some Americans are capable of expressing themselves cogently and some are not, but everybody has his own ideas on how this government of ours should be run.

At no other time and place are these peculiar opinions more likely to be given a good airing than at political gatherings. The more informal the affair, the greater the chance to corner your local representative and offer him your solutions to the problems of world affairs.

Almost everybody has sensible suggestions. Notice, I said "almost." Occasionally, one is confronted by a specimen of humanus exceptus—one of humanity's rare exceptions whose mental cogs are rotating at a speed entirely contrary to one's own.

Last Fourth of July was just such a day. Independence Day is usually filled with a host of mandated events for politicos: parades, picnics, speeches, watermelon, hot dogs, handshaking, kids, firecrackers, flags—with the festivities culminating in an appropriately inspiring display of fireworks.

People usually associate politicians with speechmaking, and rightly so. Although the exercise of the vocal cords seems to be the most common characteristic shared by politicians, you may be surprised to learn how many people think you are a great conversationalist if you listen. Or, I should say, if you appear to listen.

I try to listen visibly. It is not enough just to listen; it is important to look as if you are listening. The public servant who looks as if he is listening intently, hanging onto every word, can be mentally miles away, oblivious to what is being said. Woe unto that person who is actually listening but gives the impression that he is not. It is a surefire way to submerge one's self into constituent hot water.

Some politicians are dead-in-the-eye lookers. If a man looks you dead in the eye, you know he's listening. The trouble with the dead-in-the-eye technique is that most people become distracted by it and can't stay on the subject. It makes people very nervous. If you stare at a person's nose it isn't long before he starts wondering if he has a blemish. The same is true of his hair. I tried the hair routine for a while but noticed that it was only a matter of moments before the person with whom I was conversing started rolling his eyes upward and patting himself around the head as if looking for some foreign object.

Over the years I have developed the belt-buckle-level stare. I fix my gaze at about the belt-buckle level then turn so that I am not looking directly at my listener. I put one hand to my mouth and hold my elbow with the other hand. I try to appear as a standing replica of the statue of the Thinker.

Whenever I strike the standing Thinker pose I wait for the appropriate times to "humph." An occasional humph properly punctuates the other person's conversation and definitely shows that you are listening intently. It is important to become an expert humpher. People appreciate the attention. It is entirely probable that you have heard the same monologue a dozen times in the course of the previous twenty-four hours, but to the person with whom you are conversing, it may be the first and only opportunity to sound off to an elected official. So one must respect the singer even when he has heard the song before.

Fourth of July picnics are the worst for hearing the same thing over and over again. Everybody gets to see you for a few minutes and throughout the day you are moving, or being moved, from one group to another.

The 200th national birthday was an exception. It started out with a small-town parade that went surprisingly well. All of the antique cars in the parade functioned without a breakdown, the horses were exceptionally neat, the bands were in tune, and the American Legion Bunion Brigade was in step for most of the parade.

The only problem was the grade-school bicycle contingent. They just couldn't seem to stay in their proper place. They were in position number thirty-seven when the parade began, but by the time the parade reached its final destination at the city park, they had successfully captured position number three and were vying with the mayor's Hupmobile for number two.

I rode in a 1909 antique car with our local congressman. People smiled and waved and we waved and smiled. There were no signs on the car to identify the occupants as politicians, so we were treated most cordially. One deceived bystander shouted, "You're doing a great job. Keep it up!" Since he didn't identify which one of us he was addressing, the congressman and I split the compliment. It made my morning. The afternoon picnic was a different story.

I should have known it wouldn't be a typical Fourth of July picnic. Instead of being held in the park it was hosted by a local mortician at his home, which adjoined his place of business. In spite of the location the event was festive. The spirit of the Fourth was upon us all. I delighted the crowd by keeping my comments to less than five minutes (long-winded politicians beget short-tempered constituents at stand-up events).

Unfortunately, during the course of the afternoon, my wife

and I had become separated. Usually, Barbara sticks to me like glue, but some old schoolchums were in the audience and Barb was delightfully engaged in dusting off old memories. I found myself momentarily alone. A building was to the back of me, the beer booth to my left and a rose hedge to my right. In front of me stood a well-dressed matronly woman in her late fifties.

"Senator?" she asked.

"Yes?" I sweetly replied.

"Senator, may I talk confidentially to you for a few minutes? I have some very secret information for you."

"Humph!" I said as I lowered my head into the proper listening position. "What secrets?" I asked.

She looked to the left then moved in closer. "Senator, do you know where oil comes from?"

This gal was different. Nobody had asked me that one before. I thought everyone knew that most oil comes from holes dug in the ground. I was momentarily taken back. "Well, uh, oil comes from holes in the ground." I didn't think it was a good answer, but it was all I could muster on the spur of the moment.

"Young man," she hissed, "you don't know what you are talking about! Oil does not come from the ground, it comes from garbage!"

"Garbage?"

"Yes," she exclaimed. "Garbage! All over the United States *they* collect tons and tons of garbage, put it aboard ships and take it to the Middle East where they then process it into crude oil. Then they ship it back to us in tankers. We are being sold our own garbage at outrageous profits by the oil companies. I bet you didn't know that, did you?" She had a triumphant look on her face. She obviously knew something that this legislator didn't.

"Madam," I responded, "I hate to be argumentative, but are you sure your facts are reliable?"

"Of course I'm right! You are a senator. You should have this information too. You could go to any oil-company president and he couldn't refuse to tell *you* the truth. You could *make* him tell the truth. Oil comes from garbage!'' Her tone had changed from secretive to hostile.

I had made a boo-boo by questioning her sources. I had been in these kinds of discussions before, but never have I had my path of retreat cut off. I was cornered and she wasn't about to let me out.

''Senator, your education is obviously lacking. How can you represent your people by being such a dumb-dumb? Did you go to college?'' Before I could answer, she began again.

''It's a conspiracy, you understand. The international bankers and the Jews are working with the oil companies to cheat us all!''

I attempted to change the subject. ''You said there were 200 secrets. What are some of the others?''

It worked. She looked momentarily at the man who was working the beer booth and moved closer. In a voice saturated with authority she asked, ''Senator, do you know where water comes from?''

I felt trapped. I groped for an answer. Sweat appeared on my brow. In a voice filled with hesitation I ventured forth. ''God, maybe?''

''God!'' She shouted in a loud voice. ''Boy, are you naive! It's no wonder our country is in such a mess with ignoramuses like you in office. Your constituency should be ashamed to have such an undereducated man as their representative.''

I could feel the blood rising. I felt both sorry for her and angry. I felt sorry that she had a loose trolley and angry because of the abusive tone of her voice.

''Lady,'' I exclaimed finally, ''I am *sure* that God makes water! And I'm sure that one of us is right and the other is a candidate for the funny farm.''

She didn't hear a word I said. ''Man makes water, not God!'' she exclaimed. ''It's all done with electrical currents. Besides, you and I are God.''

Her eyes were flashing with anger. It was obvious she felt she was in the company of a lesser being.

''Madam,'' I replied, ''I believe further conversation would be a waste of your time and mine. We obviously disagree on the origin of oil and water.''

I tried to edge my way around her, but any subtle move was met by a blocking action. Finally, I feigned moving to the left and circled to the right. I was free! ''Excuse me, madam.'' I turned to speed away only to find my wife blocking further retreat.

''Is *this* man your husband?'' asked the woman of 200 secrets.

''Yes, indeed!'' beamed Barbara in her most prideful public demeanor.

''You poor dear! Do you know how uneducated your husband is? He doesn't even know where oil and water come from!''

I took the coward's way out. Before Barbara could answer, I grabbed her by the waist and jerked. I popped her from the grasp of my tormentor as a cork from a bottle. With the grace of O. J. Simpson, I weaved through the crowd, wife in tow. I paused only when I had approximately two hundred people between ourselves and the oracle.

The rest of the day I kept a respectable distance between myself and the lady with the 200 secrets. After being exposed to just two of the 200, I was determined to remain ignorant of the 198 others.

As I said in the opening of the chapter, politicians have to develop a thick skin to survive the slings and arrows and the bolts and nuts. Unfortunately, there is a fine line between a thin skin and callousness, a line that many a legislator slides across without ever knowing that it has happened to him.

9

Burros and the Pill

LEGISLATORS TEND to be fad followers. Some have a rare talent for recognizing a coming popular social movement and then circulating the story that they were one of the original gurus who conceived the idea.

Ecology is one such example. One of my colleagues humorously confided in me, "Five years ago, I couldn't spell *ecology*–now I are one!" This particular legislator's district was along the seacoast, and several colleges inhabited his bailiwick. After an oil spill along the coast, the eco-crowd on the campuses organized student protest demonstrations. Local newspapers joined in and soon the demand for legislative action was deafening.

The ecologists were up in arms. The sea had been contaminated. A number of seagulls had swum through the oily gook and were grounded. The press took a few thousand pictures of soggy birds. The papers across the state printed the story of the plight of fowl and fauna. Students demonstrated, professors denounced big business, and both indicted the decadent system that would allow such a sad situation to develop.

Bird lovers united and my colleague genuflected to the "public" pressure. He immediately introduced, with the appropriate comments, legislation he had been considering for "a long time"; his long association with, and knowledge of, ecological matters made him the best person to author the bill. The press praised his leadership, the ecology crowd accepted him as one of their legislative leaders, and the world had another instant authority.

History is replete with such examples of "leadership." The story goes that during the French Revolution a count was sitting by a window when, suddenly, a mob of people rushed by. He stood and exclaimed, "There go my people; I am their leader. I must follow them."

Unfortunately, transforming social fads into legislation can be dangerous. Somebody or some group can be irreparably harmed. Some pressure groups are expert in creating the impression that they speak for the masses when in reality they are only a vocal minority that know how to work the media.

Legislators who are subject to this kind of pressure react, and once they have committed themselves to action, become locked into the issue. Even though they would like to change, they feel committed to maintain their position. It is easier to justify a bad vote then to admit error.

I believe the ecological issue is one that the legislature has transformed into a Frankenstein. In the last six years, a great deal of injustice has been perpetrated in the name of ecology. Some legislators have blindly supported every bill with an ecology label attached.

Legislators are prone to go along because voting against "the environment" can quickly get one labeled anti–Mother Nature. To oppose an ecological issue is to be painted as a defiler of the environment, a captive of exploiting business, and a hater of future generations.

A bevy of social reformers and antibusiness special-interest groups have seized upon the ecology issue as protective coloration for their social legislation. Environment protection has been conveniently used to cover a wealth of land-management schemes.

Let me give you a tangible example. Some residents in a rural area close to Sacramento resented the fact that the area was becoming more populated. The area was, at that time, zoned for one-acre development and many people had homes on one-acre tracts. The surrounding terrain was still undeveloped, so it wasn't unusual to see a man perched on a one-acre plot with fifty acres of undeveloped land next to his property. He had, in effect, the benefit of the solitude which the undeveloped land provided.

The fifty-acre plots were rapidly being subdivided, so many of those who lived on one-acre plots got together and formed groups to protect the "outdoor environment" of their area. "We must preserve the wildlife of the area," they cried. "We must maintain green belts near our cities," they stated. "We must keep nature in its raw form whenever possible," they explained.

Their answer: Rezone the area into five-acre parcels.

Developers couldn't afford to break up the existing acreage into five-acre parcels; the market wasn't there. Many people could afford one-acre plots, as could those who were there first, but not five acres.

Do you think these local ecologists went before the local supervisors and told them the truth? Can you imagine one of them getting up and testifying that what they really wanted was the use of someone else's property without having to pay for it? Hardly! It was much simpler to become a concerned ecologist and mouth the clichés. The supervisors went along, because who wants to be against ecology? Sometimes, well-meaning do-gooders can go to extremes posing as friends of wildlife.

Several years ago the California Department of Fish and Game and several legitimate outdoor organizations came to me with a bill calling for Fish and Game Department control over wild burros. California has a lot of wild jackasses, four-legged and other. The wild variety is prolific and constitutes quite a problem to game management. They have no natural enemies and have grown disproportionately in relation to other wild desert animals.

They came to California with the prospectors and remained after the prospectors left. They foraged well, and without natural enemies, proliferated. They are ornery critters. They will chase other animals away from desert water holes and consume foliage needed for the survival of other wildlife. Maintaining a balance with the wild burros present has been difficult. The desert sheep have been severely affected by the increased burro population, since they forage off the same vegetation. Two species of desert bighorn sheep have disappeared forever because of the competition for habitat.

I was asked to introduce legislation to grant the Department of Fish and Game the authority to keep the burro population under control in proportion to the other competing species. It made sense to me, and who better to recommend it than the Department of Fish and Game?

I soon found out there were some vocal jackass lovers in California, and they were all present when my bill was presented in the Fish and Game Committee.

I was portrayed as the killer of wildlife, the destroyer of the prospector's best friend, the jackass. Didn't I have any compassion for the offspring of those noble beasts who helped to win the West? I was a murderer of California heritage, a destroyer of the desert's most lovable beastie.

One portly woman testified, "You have never lived unless you have ridden a jackass down the side of a desert mountain."

Another matronly witness was "shocked" and "horrified" that grown men could possibly contemplate the destruction of the wild burro." Our duty was to save all animals from destruction.

I asked, "How are we going to 'save' the lives of the desert sheep and deer now starving to death unless we control the burro population?"

She smiled, paused, looked at each legislator on the committee, and triumphantly stated, "Senator, we have science on our side!"

"Science?" someone asked.

"Yes, science! We now can control the birth rate with The Pill!" She beamed, obviously proud of her solution. I had some doubts that wild jenny burros would voluntarily comply with taking birth-control pills on a regular basis. Jackasses will be jackasses. I could imagine Fish and Game wardens sneaking around the desert trying to corner wild jennies with a knapsack of birth-control pills in one hand and a rope in the other and the worry of what would happen once they caught one.

After a moment of silence, one of my colleagues ventured forth, "How, madam, do you intend administering birth-control pills to a bunch of wild jackasses?"

"That's your concern," she responded. "Science has given us the solution. You should be smart enough to work out the details. Why, you could put the pills in the water holes, as one solution. I'm sure there are many others!" Without waiting for any further questions, she rose from the witness table and walked triumphantly back to her seat in the audience amidst the thunderous applause of her friends.

I managed to get my burro-control bill out of committee by a narrow vote and onto the floor of the senate. In the intervening time, the friends of the burros had been buttonholing legislators from the urban areas and had instigated a few letters in behalf of the jacks and the jennies.

When I took the bill up before the entire senate, I found myself confronted with stiff opposition from my colleagues, mainly the Democrats. I was jokingly accused of assaulting their party's symbol; they exclaimed, the "real intent of the legislation was partisan symbolism." The braying continued against my bill for what seemed to be hours. The burros became an ecological issue. Destruction of wildlife was argued. Killing of innocent animals. By the time the debate was over, the jackass had replaced the dog as man's best friend. I lost the bill handily. Few legislators were willing to grant the Fish and Game Department the power to destroy the symbol of the Democratic Party and man's best friend. The fact that the overpopulating desert jackasses were killing off other wildlife was lost in the oratory of the day.

I licked my wounds and contemplated the kicking I had

received on the floor of the senate, concluding that there were as many jackasses in Sacramento as in our deserts. The jackass population, at last count, is still growing out of control in our deserts, and, I might add, in Sacramento as well.

Probably the most symbolic *cause célèbre* of the eco-movement has been the campaign to "save" the condor. This giant throwback to prehistoric times is the feathery symbol of the ecological liberal. Maybe it is because the "save-the-condor movement" was the first genuinely successful cause advocated by the political protectionists and their friends.

Now, don't misunderstand me. I have no objection to any-one protecting anything that is dear to his heart. Folks can protect to their hearts' content any creepy thing that strikes their fancy. I believe in the right of individuals doing whatever they desire, as long as they don't step on others in the process or as long as they don't protect their "thing" with money extracted by the force of government. Some people want to protect other natural resources like gold and silver, diamonds, rubies, steel, lead, copper, or pieces of green parchment paper with engraved pictures of Presidents.

Unfortunately, liberal protectionists want to save their thing at someone else's expense. The save-the-condor movement was a classic example.

First, I think it is important to know a little about the bird. The condor is not a bird that is about to become extinct. South America and Mexico are filled with condors. It is a strong probability, however, that they would soon become extinct in California if they weren't coddled as they are. Condors are unique—they cannot exist around populated areas. They need solitude. They are so stupid that if they are disturbed by man while they are nesting, off they fly, sometimes forgetting where their nests are.

The condor is a large species of buzzard. They live off dead animals. In other words, they are scavengers. The reason for their existence was to clean up the dead carrion in the central valley of California. Before the settlers came and made the central valley an agricultural giant feeding the world's population, the valley was the haven for valley elk, deer, and grizzly bears. The condor was the huge hunchbacked scavenger vulture that cleaned up the stinking carcasses.

The condor's decline in California was in direct proportion to the human population growth. The big buzzards retreated into the foothills at the base of the San Joaquin Valley. There they could be seen soaring aloft on the connective hot-air currents of the lower valley. Except for size, they are not much more discernible from their more sociable counterpart, the vulture. Only a bird watcher could tell the difference.

Enter stage left—the save-the-condor crowd. The condor is about to become extinct! A species of wildlife will be gone forever from California!

At this point I say bravo to all the condor savers. If someone wants to save the big buzzard for posterity, be my guest! Go out and buy the land, feed them with purchased dead carrion, and garner the support of all the vulture lovers to contribute to the cause. If buzzards are one's thing, go to it! Unfortunately, the condor crowd wanted to save the bulky buzzard at someone else's expense.

The California condor is now saved. Approximately fifty of the birds exist somewhere in the primitive area close to Santa Barbara. Restricted areas are maintained for the vested vulture. Meat is purchased, at taxpayers' expense, and deposited within their private domain so they can survive. Thousands of acres are their private preserve. We spend about $200,000 a year to protect big buzzards for posterity, which, translated, means some future group of bird-watchers will have governmentally subsidized bird-watching.

If condor-watching by the public (since they pay the bill) is what's important, then I would suggest that we shoot the remaining condors and stuff them. They could then be strategically placed beside freeways around the state and more people would see the condor in five minutes than would observe them under the present circumstances within the next five hundred years. It certainly would be a lot less costly, and millions of Californians would have a chance to see what their tax dollars bought them.

Come to think of it, the condor was the best selection the protectionists could have chosen to symbolize their movement. The big prehistoric buzzard lives off carcasses. It remains aloft by soaring on hot air. It deserts its nest when confused and its defense mechanism is vomiting rotten, semidigested carrion on its opposition. The condor is a proper symbol for people who demand that their preferences be fed by the labor of others.

The ecological crowd has made the condor a motherhood issue. To attack the righteousness of a government program to save the feathery thing is tantamount to running a smear campaign against Disneyland.

Legislators bought the package and are now out to save salamanders, garden snakes, and all sorts of crawlies. It is a mark of distinction to be the author of a savior issue. We even have a group formed to protect weeds. So, whatever turns you on. . .

I have a great deal of respect for the hunter. He yearly contributes to the preservation and perpetuation of certain wildlife by the purchase of a hunting license, and voices little concern when part of the money is used to protect certain endangered species. He is putting his money up and purchasing a service in return. It is strictly voluntary.

I introduced legislation which would have allowed the protectionist the right to purchase a license for the preservation of the nongame animals. It died in the first committee. Why? The lobby against it came from . . . guess where? That's right, the eco-crowd. I am not too sure that our ecology friends are willing to put their money where their mouths are. It is much easier and personally cheaper to get some other sucker to pick up the tab—as long as we have legislators who will slavishly follow fads and finance them with taxpayers' dollars.

10

Intellectuals They Are Not

SEVERAL YEARS ago, a fellow legislator rose to deliver a written speech upon the need for fiscal integrity because of the financial "chow us" in the welfare department and "chow us" in state government. Finally it dawned upon us that it wasn't fiscal "chow us" he was reading, but "fiscal chaos." The senator obviously didn't write the speech he was giving. What's more, he didn't understand it.

There is no guarantee that the elective process will populate the legislature with intellectuals. In fact, the odds are that the campaigning and hoopla associated with attaining office will more often than not discourage those who seek intellectual fulfillment.

Legislators are usually outgoing and gregarious, not reflective and meditative.

Politicians are usually interested more in the end result than in the philosophical premises upon which they operate.

Every legislator has a philosophy, although not many understand the origin or the significance of their epistemology. There are conservatives and liberals within the legislature who can describe neither why they are what they are, nor why they think the way they do. They know what they do is "right" and "for the people" and "for the good of the country," but if asked to give the philosophical justification and the origin of their basic postulates, most could not, nor would they know where to begin.

That is not to say that there are not ideologues within the legislature, because there are. There are some deeply committed men who are articulate exponents and able practitioners of the philosophy they espouse. These men are the movers, and by the force of their convictions, they perceptibly move the laws and government in their philosophical direction—a drift which more often than not is unperceived by the bulk of the legislators who vote upon the issues.

I have heard colleagues from both parties complain, "This country's headed towards socialism," then almost with the next breath, vote for legislation that prepares for or advances some collectivist goal. Or they espouse the cause of freedom of the individual while promoting a bill that advocates more government control. Obviously, the subtleties of the legislation have totally escaped them, or these men are unmindful of the truth. Most often it is the former.

How is it that some "conservative" legislators decry big government then vote for business price-supports in the name of "free enterprise"? I suspect that these men fail to see the contradiction in their actions.

Most legislators are not intellectuals and they will freely admit it. Philosophical dissertations bore them and they will admit that too. Intellectual investigation of philosophical presuppositions can be a nervous business.

Changing ideas can be politically dangerous in the next election, so many would rather stay out of soul-searching sessions, especially with anyone who holds views contrary to their own.

Legislators often have a vested interest in ignorance. They were elected because they believed what they believed and associated with whom they associated, and to change can be dangerous to one's political health.

The invitation, "Come, let us reason together" is rarely heard. In fact, "reason" can unsettle one's psyche.

If I had to simplify by categorizing the ideologues into two basic groups, there would first of all be those who believe in the *state*, government control, management of human affairs, and see themselves as the executors of the programs and policies to regulate human behavior. The other group believes in personal and economic *freedom* for the individual, with government playing only a minor role as the peacekeeper, and the protector of individual rights.

There is a third group which naively believes that somewhere between the two, statism and personal freedom, lies euphoric philosophical middle ground, a mecca of moderation where one can pick and choose what he likes from both "extremes." Those in this group never originate ideas because their intellectual neutrality precludes them from doing so. They gravitate to the pragmatic and become the pawns of the most effective and organized of the two other groups.

The statists have the upper hand within the legislatures of America and are pushing this country closer and closer to a regulatory and redistributive system of government. Most of the actors in this social drama are reciting the lines prepared for them, happy enough to be on the stage, yet lacking the intellectual inquisitiveness to inquire about the author of the play.

11

Who Says It's Fair?

THE PUBLIC has a mistaken belief that the legislative process tends to be fair and that legislators are constantly compromising to reach equitable solutions for all parties involved.

Legislative bodies are not fair any more than a lion is fair with the lamb it has under its paw. Once in a while, a legislator will admit it.

Several years ago, a cagey old veteran senator chaired the powerful Senate Finance Committee. A witness exclaimed at one of the chairman's rulings, "Senator, that is not fair!" The senator reached over the table and tossed to the witness a copy of *Mason's Manual*, the rules which govern the parliamentary actions of the senate.

"Show me, sir," asked the chairman, "where it says we have to be fair."

He was absolutely right. A fairness doctrine is not written into any of the rules of how the legislature operates.

"But," you may ask, "doesn't the legislature want to be fair?" Fair about what? If Senator Zilchovitch wants to get the state into the housing construction industry, and you believe the state has no moral right to be in direct competition with the construction industry, what is there to compromise? Building only one-story buildings?

If Senator Barfnoble wants to take money from hard workers and give it to nonworkers, what's fair? Taking only a little bit? Since when does the burglar have a right to compromise with you over how much he steals from your home?

Senator Sweetloaf believes government employees have a right to strike, and you don't. What is to negotiate? Strike only on weekends?

For all these examples, there can be no compromise or legislative fairness. There are many areas of legislation where fairness is only relative to one's basic premises. If one believes, as does Senator Zilchovitch, that government should duly compete with business, then the debate or compromise can only concern the degree of intervention into the private sector.

If one believes, as does Senator Barfnoble, that government has the right to redistribute the wealth, take from the haves and give to the have-nots, then it is an easy matter to be "fair." The debate, then, is only over who gets plundered, how much, and who receives the loot.

If one believes, as does Senator Sweetloaf, that public employees have a right to strike, then it is only a question of how large a payoff is equitable in getting them to stay on the job.

Whenever government assumes the role of regulator of human activity and redistributor of wealth, then the question of fairness is not even a topic to be discussed. Fairness flies out the window. It becomes a matter of who has the power and how much can be gotten away with at any given time.

The legislator who would like to see government manage all businesses and regulate all human behavior is constantly introducing legislation toward that end. Every year that he succeeds in getting even a small particle of it into law is a successful year. He is just that much further ahead of last year. A pygmy could consume an elephant if he were willing to do it a piece at a time.

Unless the ground rules are set down on what the legislature is to do (job description), and as long as the public accepts the false assumption that with a majority of votes the legislature can do as it pleases, there can be no fairness or justice in how the legislature accomplishes its tasks.

Justice and fairness presuppose equality of treatment for all.

But, how is justice possible when a majority can use government to take advantage of a minority? How can fairness prevail when numerical superiority is the criterion for legislative action?

Just because a bill becomes law does not make it fair or just. That it has made its tortuous way through the legislative process is no guarantee of its morality. There is no moral magic in majorities, nor is logical consistency assured for a vociferous minority.

The control of most legislative bodies around America now resides in the hands of those who believe in increased government ownership and management of human affairs. This fact is so obvious, it hardly bears stating. One need look only at the legislative committee system for confirmation.

A man may be an expert in a given field and never be assigned to a committee where his expertise can be employed. If he is of a philosophical persuasion contrary to that of the leadership, then, tough toast. Key committee appointments are usually made on the basis of partisan flavor rather than expertise.

If, as an example, there were six legislators whose philosophy of education were contrary to that of the house leadership, would they be on the education committee in sufficient numbers to affect policy? Small chance. The party line inevitably takes precedence over knowledge of the subject. A legislator's request for a committee assignment is sometimes granted, but never if his selection will gum up the philosophical direction of the incumbent leadership.

A great deal of lip service is given to the "nonpartisan" nature of legislative bodies once the election is over. In fact, some solons say it so often they start to believe it. But the cold, hard facts are, the spoils of war go to the victor; and in politics, the choice committees go to those who adhere to the party line. Whatever tidbits are tossed to the losers are usually reserved for those who will play ball with the winners.

Does it stand to reason that the leadership, in order to be

fair, would assign power positions to those who would dismantle programs the leadership has implemented? Hardly! In fact, the contrary is usually the case.

Every angle is implemented to make sure that the most formidable and talented opponent gets the dregs and leftovers. The politically astute rarely expose their flanks to the opposition, nor are they willing to give a platform to their philosophical enemies.

So, in our present legislative system, what is "fair"? Whatever can be gotten away with. What else?

12

Peer-Group Shift

A MOST FRUSTRATING experience is to vote for a man whom you believe to be Joe Goodguy, only to find that once elected, he turns into Senator Twoface. If I've been asked the question once, I've been asked a hundred times, "What happened? I thought he was Joe Goodguy when I voted for him."

"He probably was," I would reply. "In all probability, he's been victimized by the peer-group shift."

"The peer-group what?"

"Peer-group shift. Your pal Joe has replaced his hometown peers for a different group of acquaintances. He shifted friendships and loyalties. The peer-group shift can happen to any solon, especially since the advent of year-round legislatures. The modern trend is for the local hero to have less and less contact with his peer group back in the district."

Let me show how it works. Joe Goodguy is encouraged by his friends (peer group) to run for office. Joe has been active in local affairs and many people know him to be an honest, good fellow. Heeding the call, Joe runs and wins. The major issue of his campaign is tax relief. Joe campaigns to cut back spending, especially in the administrative costs of government. Local people rally to the call and send their victorious knight off to the capital to slay bureaucratic dragons.

Not long after he arrives in the capital, he is given the opportunity to meet the lobbyist of one of the many governmental employee groups. Now, how do you visualize a lobbyist who represents governmental employees? A radical with a beard? An erudite intellectual? No, the lobbyist could easily pass for a beer salesman from one of the local breweries.

In this case, he does. A ruddy-complexioned, happy, affable Irishman by the name of Mike lobbies for the employee group. He greets our hero with a warm smile and a friendly handshake, and is all ears to our hero's complaints.

After our newly elected dragon slayer has vented his spleen on the employee representative, instead of an argument, the pleasant Irishman completely concurs. "I agree with you, sir. It has been a deplorable situation. There is *much* bureaucracy which has to be cut back. *Responsible* government employees (which I represent) heartily concur. Let's go have a beer and talk it over."

It is not very long before newly elected Joe Goodguy runs out of complaints and is hearing "the other side" over a few frosties at one of the local bistros frequented by the lobbyists and the legislature. Four beers later, they are on "Joe" and "Mike" terms.

"Joe," says Mike, "I hear you like to hunt. I just happen to be a member of a great duck club. Why don't you come down this weekend and we can discuss this matter in a more relaxed atmosphere."

Joe loves to hunt, so he accepts. Many beers and a few duck hunts later (at a club that Joe could hardly afford), our hero has a slightly different outlook on government employee matters. Mike has told him all about it. By this time, Mike and the other lobbyists have blown enough smoke into Joe's ear that his hat hardly fits his swollen head.

Back in the district, Joe's supporters are more disappointed each day, especially when there is no action from Joe. They are not as understanding as Mike, the lobbyist. Why should they be? They're not paid $80,000-plus a year to snuggle up to Joe. Their approach is, "Joe, why in the heck aren't you doing what we sent you to the capital to do? Our taxes are getting higher and higher, and you are not speaking out as you once did against the evils of bureaucracy.''

Joe replies, ''But you people don't understand the whole picture. It's a lot more complex than it appears on the surface. The representatives of governmental employees are well aware of the problems, and within the scope of civil-service fairness, human rights, and equal opportunity, they are trying to handle the situation to everyone's satisfaction.''

''Handle it!'' shouts Joe's original backers. ''The state just hired more personnel while the taxpaying sector is suffering through a recession. They are also demanding a pay increase along with added vacation benefits!'' It is a stormy session.

Joe retreats to the capital, bloodied by his district peer group and his pride wounded. He is their representative—how dare they treat him in such a manner!

Back at the capital, who is there to console Joe? Who is ready, willing, and able to replace the hometown donors with matching contributions? Who else? Why, old buddy Mike, that's who.

It is not long before Joe is having dinner at the home of the president of the Government Employees Association and being served in first-class style. Once an enemy of bureaucratic mismanagement, Joe is now a friend of civil service.

Peer-group shift. New friends replacing old. New friends who contribute to your campaigns, buy your dinners, treat you like a king. And once you are their friend, they do what they can to keep you in office—that is, until they find someone whom they can manipulate more easily.

The ratio of registered lobbyists to legislators across America is in excess of five to one. The vast majority are extremely charming, delightfully entertaining, and filled with concern over your well-being. They laugh at all your jokes and are seemingly imperturbable. They are your buddies, at least as long as you are in the legislature.

Their stock-in-trade is getting to know elected officials intimately—to sway opinion. The better they are at their jobs, the more money they make. Their product is charm. Their profession is persuasion.

The hometown constituent is a poor match for the smiling professional, especially if the legislator spends the majority of his time in the capital.

Another peer-group shift can take place with legislative colleagues, regardless of party. Good ole Joe discovers that members of the opposition party don't actually have fangs and are, in many cases, a great bunch of fellows.

If Joe isn't particularly well grounded in his philosophy, it isn't long before he tries to be a "good ole boy" to all of his colleagues. Usually this means that Joe becomes susceptible to a request to vote for a fellow solon's legislation.

The temptation is strong. The more time Joe spends with his colleagues and the less time he spends at home, the greater the urge to "help" his newfound peers. Even for those whose philosophical base is strong, the temptation is always there to please a fellow legislator.

Every legislator has some binding ties to other members. The very fact that legislators have successfully survived the elective process gives them something in common; an experience that few can appreciate who have not been through the same grind.

All of this, and more, binds some men very tightly to the legislative fraternity. After a while, the "club" can become very important in the life of a legislator, and the opinions of club peers more important than the principles upon which good ole Joe was elected.

Joe finds it increasingly difficult to point the accusing finger at bad legislation, because the author of the bill was Joe's dinner companion the evening before, or will be his fishing partner next week.

The advent of the full-time, year-round legislature compounds the problem, making Joe more and more susceptible to programs and legislation which tend to give incumbents an advantage. Since Joe's home base has deteriorated, his financial well-being is directly dependent upon his legislative job. Under these circumstances, Joe finds it easier and easier to justify using the powers of his office to promote his incumbency.

"I wonder what happened to good ole Joe . . .?"

If Joe was actually a good guy when he left home, chances are he has become the victim of peer-group shift.

13

Too Many Lawyers

THERE IS A ritual that every legislator goes through at least once a week; it happens during a first introduction.

"Charlie, I'd like you to meet Senator Fuzzdubble!" Senator Fuzzdubble smiles and extends his hand. The person to whom he is introduced raises one eyebrow, keeps his hand to his side, leans forward, sticks his chin out, and asks, "Are you a lawyer?"

If one says no, then the person smiles, extends his hand, and usually makes some uncomplimentary remark about politics in general and lawyers in particular. Although lawyers are not too popular today, they dominate the legislative halls.

Politics and lawyers go together like Mexico and Montezuma's revenge. It is only logical to expect those who make their living "interpreting" the law to show an interest in writing it.

A good argument can be made that the very fact that lawyers are lawyers makes them unsuitable for the task of forming moral judgments, the very fabric of law.

I don't want it to appear that I'm prejudiced against all lawyers, because I am not. One married my sister; I've gone to the same schools with them; why, I've even eaten with them on occasion—but I don't think I want so many of them living next door at the capital.

Lawyers are influenced by their environment and their legal peers. Their training in law school, combined with the nature of their business, causes them to approach life in a manner quite distinct from the way the rest of us do.

It is rumored that every law school has secret courses that are required for graduation. Namely, Obtuse Language, Know-It-All, and Preconditioned Avoidance. The first, Obtuse Language, requires a student to take perfectly understandable English sentences and rewrite them in such a way that, without difficulty, none, save lawyers, can understand them. They have succeeded beyond their wildest dreams. Not only is the general population confused, but so are other lawyers. They will spend hours and days analyzing what one lawyer has said, trying to discover the intent. Just when they think they have it all figured out, along come nine lawyers called the Supreme Court who divide the issue five to four.

The second course is Know-It-All. This instills in the psyche of each future member of the bar that belief that he is a member of a superior race, and above all the intellectual machinations of us commoners.

The third secret course taught in law school is Preconditioned Avoidance. This is the course where the law school students are conditioned (like Pavlovian pooches) never, never to make a statement without leaving a backdoor open. They cannot pass this course until it is a conditioned reflex.

After the young students complete these three courses, rumor has it that they take an oath never to let the public know about the three cornerstones of lawyerdom.

I'm convinced that part of the secret ritual is also to swear upon a volume of Blackstone never to speak unkindly in public of a brother counselor, socialize with any colleague who dares to run against an incumbent judge, or give a direct answer to any question asked by an infidel (nonlawyer).

All joking aside, I find that many people assume that lawyers make good legislators because of their legal training. They mistakenly believe that understanding how to read the law is the most important part of being a good legislator. There is no question that it helps in reading legislation. Lawyers have drafted most of the legislation on the books today and it helps to be aware of the language of law.

But—legislating is primarily a moral act and only second-arily a technical task. A man who is elected to office has been chosen by people in all walks of life, not just the legal profes-sion, and the man elected usually makes campaign promises on how he will morally handle the office that he seeks. Lawyers are smart enough to recognize this, and when they seek your vote, do they promise, "I'll draft technically better laws for you"? Hardly. They campaign on issues, as other candidates do.

Think about it. Is the abortion issue a technical question or a moral judgment? How about capital punishment? School cur-ricula? While some speciously contend that "you can't legis-late morality," the fact is that you can't legislate anything else. The vast majority of important issues that face the legis-lator are matters of philosophical, moral judgment. He puts his philosophy and morals on the line when he votes, not his technical knowledge of the law. Is it good or bad?—that is the question. The legal technology is of secondary importance.

If one accepts the premise that the votes a legislator casts are primarily philosophical, then one might conclude, as I do, that lawyers are not the best persons to represent the people.

Why do I say that? Let us look at the nature of the legal profession for the answer. Most lawyers are for hire. Their services are sold, as in any other service profession, to the client who can afford them.

The lawyer's problem is the client's problem. It is his responsibility when he takes the case to represent the desires of his client and to counsel him. Whenever a person needs a lawyer it is often because somebody else has already gotten one.

The contemporary ethic of the modern-day counselor is to provide good representation for a fee, not to question whether his client is right or wrong, but to give his client the best technical assistance available. Lawyers, like others, try not to involve themselves emotionally in their client's problems.

It is not unheard of to have a lawyer representing two

different clients before two different courts where he is on both sides of the same issue, where in one court he is arguing A against B, and in the other B against A.

Can you imagine a lawyer being financially successful if, after a potential client walked into his law office and presented his case, the lawyer responded, "I think you're dead wrong and don't you think you are being unfair? The settlement you are asking for is really ridiculous, and even though you might get it, you're taking undue advantage of the other side!"

How long would that lawyer last? I can tell you, he wouldn't be part of a going law firm for long. Lawyers find it unprofitable to come to conclusions and make moral decisions when selecting clients.

A lawyer lives in his professional world—a universe of arbitration, conflict, and compromise. Today's FOR is tomorrow's AGAINST. Add to this the lack of emotional commitment to his client's case. A counselor maintains the attitude of a doctor toward his patient—emotional neutrality. It is financially unwise to make a personal commitment on an issue.

Legal beagles often believe that personal involvement could warp their ability properly to handle the case. Personal, emotional involvement has a tendency to prejudice a counselor's judgment, especially during courtroom proceedings.

Emotion is thought to be a courtroom tool—something which one uses rather than something which uses one. It is indecorous for a lawyer to get upset. A lawyer may become emotional during a court proceeding, but, more often than not, it is a planned outbreak, designed to achieve a certain impact upon the jury or a witness.

After lawyers spend years developing this professional attitude, they tend to have recognizable habit patterns. Personal ethics become quite subjective; conclusions are avoided.

When elected to office, these habits are not discarded. Having represented both sides of many issues for years, many lawyers assume the posture of judges rather than representatives. They attend committees and evaluate the information presented. They listen to the pros and cons, then make their decision. If a bill has no opposition, they usually vote for it.

This is exemplified by one hearing held before the senate's Committee on Education. All of the teachers' lobby groups, the special-interest groups in education, and a legion of representatives from the Department of Education were on hand to introduce hundreds of millions of dollars' worth of new educational programs they wished to implement. They all were in harmony over the "need" for these new programs. Nobody came before the committee to argue against them or against increased expenditures; no tax group was in evidence, no citizens' group on fiscal responsibility in education— nobody.

After the proponents argued their case, the chairman asked if there was any opposition to the proposed legislation. Of course, there was none. I asked as many questions as I could, enough to satisfy my mind that these programs weren't justified. The vote was taken and I was the only no vote in the committee.

After the committee hearing was over, I was walking down the corridors with one of the members of the Education Committee, a fellow Republican and lawyer.

"You know, Bill," he said, "it is too bad that the people don't have anybody up here to represent them before committee."

"What the heck do you think you are?" I responded.

See my point? My colleague looked upon himself as a judge, not as a representative fighting for the fiscal rights of his constituency. He felt he was a judge viewing both sides and then casting a vote. Since there was no opposition, only "evidence" presented by the proponents, his vote was aye.

Some lawyers have a tough time coming to conclusions. Conclusions are born from assessing facts, weighing them in accordance with one's philosophy, then acting upon those facts.

Since philosophy to lawyers is financially cumbersome,

they usually develop only enough of it to survive in a world that sometimes requires conclusions.

Legal beagles enjoy all the technical aspects of legislation, often spending hours nitpicking. They oftentimes become so engrossed in the details that the substance of the legislation is forgotten or bypassed.

We need more nonlawyers in the legislature. Men whose avocation demands hard facts and whose success is predicated on the ability to form conclusions.

14

Restitution, Regulation, and Redistribution

PEOPLE MAKE a mistake when they pay their legislators good salaries, expect them to work full time, and then complain about all the governmental intervention in their lives. Do we get mad when a jackass brays or a pigeon decorates a statue? So, why become irate when legislators do their thing?

The nature of legislators is to legislate, and that is what they do. They work full time introducing new bills that create more agencies, bureaus, commissions, and regulatory functions of government. They believe that this is what is expected of them, and as long as the public expects legislators to make laws, they will.

One must remember that laws are not just friendly suggestions on how people should act; each carries with it the full force of the police power of the state. Refusing to adhere to the letter of the law is punishable by fines or trips to the Crowbar Motel. Just willfully break some regulation, and see how long it takes the police powers of the legislature to punish your indiscretion.

Laws can be divided into three different categories. I call them the three Rs—restitution, regulation, and redistribution.

Restitution is the fundamental premise of both our criminal and civil laws. If the person or property of a citizen is injured or damaged, our Judeo-Christian and English common-law heritage holds that government should apprehend the offender and hold him responsible for his actions. The simple justice of

79

this system is sometimes not readily apparent to the modern mind, conditioned as it is to such phrases as "crimes against society" and "social justice."

Although crime was indeed regarded as a sin against God, restitution was made directly to the victim. When a fine was imposed or a period of servitude required, the money did not flow into the coffers of the state, nor was the labor diverted to penal institutions to paint license plates. Any consideration extracted from the criminal accrued to the victim or the victim's family.

Before casting this concept aside as barbaric and outmoded, let us first consider the present state of affairs in our criminal-justice system. Current judicial thought holds the criminal responsible for a "crime against society." Society, or the state, is the victim; and, when a fine is paid, it is the state which receives the benefit. The actual victim is looked upon as nothing more than a witness. Instead of restitution for his loss, the victim instead must pay taxes to feed and clothe the criminal while he works off his "debt to society" in prison.

The older idea of restitution places an actual value on the damage or injury, and thus the punishment fits the crime in a very real sense. The current concept of crimes against "society," however, has made any genuine restitution to the actual victim virtually impossible. Since criminals are not held specifically accountable for their crimes, we have created an entire class of criminals for whom crime pays, figuratively and literally.

Before the advent of societal crime, those who refused to make restitution or those who habitually victimized their neighbors did indeed suffer punishment. But for the great mass of those committing crimes, rather than to languish in a jail cell, the opportunity was given to "make right" offenses.

By permitting the offender the opportunity to work productively to clear his record and his conscience, the system made restitution to the victim, punished the offender in proportion to his crime, and provided rehabilitative services superior to those found in our current criminal-justice system. By comparison, our current practices look like a twentieth-century version of debtors' prison.

Since our present system has had the effect of creating a class of career criminals, we accomplish little more through incarceration than fattening up our thieves and murderers for another foray into the community. Most are not rehabilitated. They suffer no remorse. And, needless to say, unless capital punishment serves as the ultimate sentence for the habitual offender and incorrigible, no system of restitution, whether it be incarceration and payment of fines to the state or payment or service to the victim, can effectively control the criminal population and maintain peace and order in the community. Instead of leaving both criminal and victim bitter, as does our current system, restitution tempers justice with mercy.

Although the abandonment of this concept of restitution has been most evident in our criminal laws, the growing judicial practice of assigning liability where there has been no fault threatens to spread the medical "malpractice" dilemma into every area of our civil law. If that occurs, then the last bastion of lawful restitution will have been sacrificed to the advocates of "social" justice.

This concept of social justice, by denying individual fault, denies individual responsibility. It should come as no surprise, then, to find that as the principles of individual liberty and restitution wane, the two other Rs—regulation and redistribution—come increasingly into play.

Regulatory laws are founded upon the premise that government has the right, as well as the social responsibility, to prevent people from performing certain acts. You-can't-build-this-high-unless-you-build-this-wide laws. You-can't-mix-this-glop-with-this-gook laws. You-can't-ratchet-this-unless-you-remedy-that laws. You-can't-teach-this-unless-that-regulation-is-met laws. Regulatory laws are laws that deny elbowroom.

Legislative authors always have a good reason for proposing such laws and the "public" is always the beneficiary—so they think. But, inevitably, somebody is told he can't do what he was doing before, unless some agency or bureau gives him approval.

Governmental do-gooders love to regulate; they love to protect us from ourselves. Regulation appeals to the mother instinct, not to mention the egos of legislators and bureaucrats alike. Since they know what's best for us, it stands to reason they must protect their "children" from harm. They view man as a purely social animal, who has neither responsibility for his actions nor a claim to inalienable freedoms.

Regulating human behavior is very tempting to legislators. It makes us feel so noble. Legislative nobility has been responsible for laws that prohibit people from skydiving while drunk. We regulate how sweet a grape must be before it can be sold, the sizes of boxes in which all produce is shipped, and even the amount of water permissible in toilet bowls. Next we probably will regulate how many times one may flush.

Whenever government really gets rolling on the regulation road, someone always gets hurt; individuals suffer, often those who are incapable of fighting back. As an example, let me tell you about Carl Forsberg, chicken plucker from Auburn.

Carl Forsberg is a man in his early sixties—independent, proud and a distinct individualist. Mr. Forsberg is also a cripple, and many normal avenues of employment are therefore restricted to him. However, as it is with most Americans of his generation, ingenuity is practically a part of his character. With the help of friends he constructed on the back of his property a three-room shack. The structure was not beautiful, but it was functional enough to house the equipment Carl had bought. The machinery was chicken-plucking equipment. Carl Forsberg had gone into the chicken-plucking business.

Anyone who has ever had the experience of relieving fowl of their feathers will testify that it is an occasion not soon forgotten—a foul experience, if you will pardon the pun. I have yet to find a person who takes delight in it, but many people do things because of economic necessity. To Carl, it was a financial decision. It was either plucking chickens or becoming a ward of the public.

It wasn't long before many people in the Auburn area frequented Carl's business and several of the restaurants came to him for his services. His final product was a plucked chicken, clean and neat, placed in a cellophane bag, twenty-five cents a bird. Carl wasn't prosperous, but at least he wasn't standing in the welfare line.

Enter villain—stage left, the Division of Public Health, Department of Agriculture, protector of the people. It seems that the department, in 1968, raised its standards concerning what constituted a sanitary chicken-plucking house; and, alas, Carl's homemade establishment did not meet the new regulations. In order to comply with the suggested changes made by the department, it would have cost Mr. Forsberg thousands of dollars. There were cracks in the cement floor, his wiring was exposed in some places, the refrigeration unit was not what the department liked, etc.; so Mr. Forsberg was asked to bring his establishment up to standards or shut his doors to business.

Mr. Forsberg, in order to comply with the law, closed down. But now this rugged individual from Auburn was caught between the proverbial rock and the hard place. He still abhorred welfare. He enjoyed being his own man and friends still came to him wanting him to clean their chickens. They were not concerned about department standards because they knew he kept his place extremely clean, cracked floors and all. So Mr. Forsberg, against the restrictions of the Department of Agriculture, plucked a few chickens for friends who wanted his services. The paradox is that the regulations allowed Mr. Forsberg to pluck wild birds, pheasants, ducks, quail, and geese, but somehow or other forbade him from picking domesticated birds. The distinction may seem somewhat obscure to you and me, but not to the minds of the Department of Agriculture's Division of Public Health.

It was not long before the government found out about his

undercover chicken plucking, so public-health officials hauled him before the court and he was ordered to desist. He was breaking the law, it was stated. The court gave him the proverbial slap on the wrist.

Not long afterward, and again out of the kindness of his heart, he accepted a deal from a friend. If Carl would clean some birds, in exchange for his services he could keep half of them to feed his family. He accepted the offer; no money was being exchanged. Unfortunately, Carl was caught cleaning the chickens. He was arrested. This time the judge fined him $200 or ten days in jail. Mr. Forsberg did not have the $200, so he spent ten days in the county jail. His crime? Plucking chickens for a friend. The offense? Breaking a government regulation.

Was anyone hurt by Mr. Forsberg's actions? No. Were people forced to use his services? No. In fact, they wanted Carl to clean their chickens. It is a sorry state of affairs when an American citizen can be jailed like a common criminal for performing a service others desire while harming no one in the process.

I believe the tail feathers have been plucked on that proud eagle that represents this country. Can one doubt that Americans are going to regulate themselves right out of their freedoms if the direction in which the bureaucracy is headed is not altered? Have not other nations strangled themselves to death in rules and regulations purportedly enacted to protect their citizens? The case of Carl Forsberg should be a warning to all.

Lying beneath the façade of "public good" that comes from governmental regulations lurk the special interests which prosper from governmental intervention and restrictions.

Mediocre corporations and businesses find that regulating competition out of existence is sometimes far easier than competing in the marketplace. The free market has its perils and many large bureaucratic corporations, fearing competition from smaller, more efficient competitors, seek regulations and standards to which they alone can adhere.

Some businessmen find it "convenient" for government to

regulate facets of their industry for the advantage of some within their profession. Standardization is the watchword. Businessmen naively believe they can control the governmental commissions they help create, but inevitably, the regulatory agency grows and grows until it is questionable who controls whom. The question is ultimately answered to the dissatisfaction of all, save the government bureaucracy.

Many businesses recognize that regulations are convenient tools for controlling competition. Here's a classic case of regulating competitors.

Many years ago, some segments of California agriculture asked the legislature to control the size of *all* containers used to ship fruits and vegetables, right down to the slat size on the boxes. Standardization was the reason given. If a grower wanted to ship cantaloupes to market in a bigger crate, for instance, he would have to get a bill passed allowing him to do so.

One poor soul had the misfortune to be inventive. He successfully experimented and developed a larger cauliflower. It was a superior product. He came to the Department of Agriculture to request permission to ship his product to the eastern markets in a larger box. The standard box was too small for three heads across and too big for two heads. A temporary permit was granted. His product was a smashing success! The next year he had his local senator introduce a bill to allow him to continue using the larger crate. His bill was defeated.

Why? you ask. Simple. His competitors couldn't grow a cauliflower as large as his, and since there were more of them than there was of him, they implored their legislators to defeat the bill—which they did. The consumer will never have the opportunity to buy this cauliflower because the inventive farmer went back to growing the standard sizes. The housewife, to this day, doesn't know she was denied a better product because of regulations.

Regulatory laws have been used to control competition from

time immemorial. Associations, unions, businessmen, pressure groups, do-gooders—all love the regulatory laws of government. They can restrict and modify behavior to fit their norms. Americans have become so accustomed to accepting the regulatory function of government that they hardly question the rightness of regulatory laws or the legitimacy of government's "right to regulate."

The more I see of government intervention, the surer I am that America would be better off if we abolished *all* regulatory laws, took our chances with a few who would take advantage of the lack of regulation, and then stiffened our laws on fraud and bunko. In other works, sock it to the merchant or worker who deceives, cheats, and defrauds, but leave the vast number of citizens alone from the stifling impact of governmental regulations. I'm sure that the consumer would be better off in the long and short run. True competition and free entry into the labor market soon would bring prices down for the consumer—not to mention the vast saving in taxes paid to run the governmental agencies that oversee all the regulatory laws.

The third type of law is the worst—redistribution of the wealth. These laws are the ones that attract most of the special-interest groups to the legislative halls—organizations, special lobbying groups, governmental beneficiaries—to make sure they get their share of the loot, or, conversely, to make sure they do not pick up the tab.

Redistributive laws take from one group and (as the legislators see fit) give to some other group. They are properly called nest-feathering laws. Somebody's nest gets the feathers from some plucked taxpayer; or put another way, one group gets the nest and the other gets the bird.

People shouldn't confuse redistributive laws with taxes imposed for direct services received by the public.

Nobody complains too loudly about taxes when they are the direct beneficiaries, as in the case of fire and police protection, a municipal sewage system, or water district. Taxes are usually proportionate to the use, and the taxpayer can see the direct benefit to himself and his family.

The major tax inequities are inevitably in areas where there is no measurable direct benefit to the taxed—welfare, food stamps, education, foreign aid, and a myriad of other social programs designed to redistribute wealth from the haves to the have-nots—to the plucker from the pluckee. Redistributive laws are responsible for over two-thirds of all governmental taxation.

The vast number of today's politicians see themselves as the arbitrators overseeing who gets what from whom and who keeps how much of what's left. Unfortunately, the public has grown to accept the socialist premise that redistributing the wealth *is* the function of representative government; and if the elected government takes from one to give to another, then it is moral. Somehow, the process of passing a law makes that which was immoral, moral. Somehow, when a majority of those elected vote affirmatively to allow one group to plunder another, legitimacy is conferred upon an act once deemed thievery. Redistributive government is an alien concept to those who profess freedom of individual rights, and such government is repugnant once it is understood.

Suppose I asked someone to set aside money for his medical benefits and he refused, and then suppose I pulled a weapon and forced him to contribute, I would, quite properly, be regarded as a thief, a blackguard, a tyrant, a robber, and a brute. But—and here's the fascinating part—if I were an elected official and did the same thing, I would be regarded as a socially responsible humanitarian.

In both cases the principle is the same; one is just more personal than the other. Both use force, both have an unwilling contributor, both have the same goal.

When government plunders, it does so on such a grand scale that the expropriated feel comfort that they haven't been the only ones singled out. Also, when one's own government plunders, one tends to justify the forcible act as a "necessary" use of police power. Although the dollar amount may be the same in both areas, the government establishes a system of thievery that is semipainless (withholding) so the theft is never completely understood or observed. The plunder is then wrapped in the swaddling clothes of humanitarianism, and the exploited are cast in the role of being against security or health if they object too loudly.

What is involved is a fundamental concept of justice. Let me ask you, the reader, three simple questions.

1. Do you believe someone has a right to improve his own lot at your expense? Put another way, do you believe someone has a right to feather his nest with your feathers?

If you answered no, then you are to be applauded. No one has a "right" to that which belongs to you. Conversely, you have no right to that which someone else has earned through his peaceful endeavors.

2. Do you believe someone has a right to feather another's nest at your expense?

If you answered no, you are right again. Just because a third party is the beneficiary of that which has been taken from you doesn't remove the taker from the role of a plunderer.

Put it in a more contemporary light: Does an Australian aborigine have a right to anything an American lawfully owns? Does a Canadian Indian have a right to any wealth legitimately accumulated by an Israeli Jew? The answer is obvious. No. Then, why should an affluent American black be forced to support an unproductive southern white? Or why should any-one be forced to support another? There is no moral right for me to benefit at the expense of others.

Let's understand one thing. Every person has a personal, moral obligation to help those less fortunate, but the ultimate decision to do so resides with the one who is the owner of the disposable commodity.

3. Do you believe that might makes right? That strength constitutes righteousness? If you replied no, then bravo again. Might has never been a guarantee of righteousness. That a man has greater strength than a woman gives him no right to impose his will upon her. Likewise, that there are more of us than of you, doesn't make us right. Might, whether strength of arms or

sheer numerical superiority, does not by itself constitute right.

So, let's put them together. Does a majority vote make right the actions of the legislature to take from one and give to another?

If you think so, perhaps you should take another look at your premises. Because if you believe that the majority has that right, you should not be surprised when all that you possess (including your life) falls subject to the arbitrary power of the men the majority elects.

15

A Full Time Legislature—Yuk!

IF THERE IS a subtle message in this book it is the following. Listen carefully.

DON'T EVER LET YOUR STATE GO TO A FULL TIME LEGISLA-TURE. IF YOU DO, YOU WILL LIVE TO REGRET IT!

In 1966, Californians bought the propaganda that the Golden State needed a full time legislature. It was promoted by liberal legislators, lobbyists and a host of citizenry who thought they were doing the right thing. I have to admit, it all sounded so good. The media was filled with comments like: "There is too much work for a part time legislator." "How can we hope to attract good men to government when we pay them such a trivial amount!" "The special interests will have less impact on a legislator if he receives a decent salary." "Full time legislators can keep a better check on the executive branch if they work at it full time." And, "In the long run it will cost us less because a full time legislature will know better when to cut and trim."

I could give you a whole bunch of extra reasons given on why Californians bought the full time farm—eggs, turkeys, and all—but why bother. It was a big costly mistake.

The quality of our legislature has gone downhill ever since. The cost of our state government has gone from a three billion budget in 1966 to an eighteen billion budget in twelve years, and get this, eight of those twelve years was under the Reagan administration and four under a fairly fiscally conservative Democrat (Brown).

90

The legislators today are younger, more liberal and fiscally irreverent. One feels that they are trying to spend it all before the money evaporates. They are mindful of a young lad who was painting a wall furiously. When asked why he was painting so fast he responded that he wanted to finish before the paint gave out. Our present legislature is an ingenious bunch when it comes to finding new sources of revenue. They are busily seeking new areas to tax. The governmental beast needs to be fed and his appetite is only satiated by green pieces of parchment with the engraved images of presidents thereon.

We tax you for everything in California. You can bet that if it's stationary or moving it has some kind of tax on it. Even when you die we get you by sticking your heirs for what you left. We have sales tax, income tax, property tax, excise tax, business tax, inventory tax, capital gains tax, transfer tax, plus scores of others. We even have, "if you would'a" taxes. That's a tax on if you would'a used that so and so, you would'a paid, but since you don't and could'a, we will tax you anyway.

We have an army of people engaged in collecting taxes from Californians and any out-of-stater who slows down enough to tag. Most of this budgetary monstrosity is the product of our full time legislature and all the new young turks that gravitated to legislative service since 1966.

Let's take one of the points that sold the California taxpayer on the full time legislature—"The work load is too heavy for a part time legislator." Heavy or not, they got it all done. If the load was too heavy the obvious answer was to introduce and pass fewer laws, not expand the time the legislature stayed in session. But that's what happened with the advent of a full time body of busy-bee legislators—with more time, more laws were introduced. To accommodate the workload, the committee systems were changed so that it became easier to get a bill passed. Fewer committee bills died, so the amount of time needed to keep up on all the bills increased proportionately. People expected more from a full time legislator so extracurricular engagements became more pronounced. It became more difficult to turn down speaking engagements or requests for bill introduction. The job became the sole source of revenue for many legislators. After a while, legislators became *more* dependent upon the job than before, thus powerful special interest groups were listened to a little more intently. The longer he is a full time legislator, the more dependent he becomes upon his salary. His former occupation and its business contacts are in the past and difficult to re-establish; going back to his old occupation seems like a step backward. It becomes all the more important to keep his legislative job and whatever retirement benefits that have accrued. Keeping the job becomes a matter of personal survival. Whenever the job becomes more important to a legislator than the issues on which he votes, he is no longer a worthy representative. His own security outranks judgment.

One of the beauties of a part time legislature is that the office is more likely to be kept in proper perspective. The world doesn't come to an end if a legislator is deposed. It was part time, the pay wasn't good enough to support a man and his family, so those who ran for office *had to be successful in other fields of endeavor*. His perspective was broader because he was not only a legislator but a taxpayer as well. He inevitably had to go back into his community for most of the year and live with the laws he had passed. Local peer group pressure was ever present. Once he became a full time legislator, all that changed. Local peer group influence diminished as he spent more and more time in the state capital. It was only a matter of time before a professional politician became your representative and as a professional, he spent an inordinate amount of his time figuring out how to perpetuate himself in office.

There is now a type who gravitates to government like fungus does to a damp, dark corner. These are the social hot shots, the do-gooders, the social reformers, the planners, the philanthropists with the public pocketbook. Our state colleges and universities are graduating them by the carloads. They are trained to enter governmental service and to revolutionize our democratic process. Governmental service is their goal, their ideal. They enter the bureaucracy believing in planning, ecology and welfare rights. They descend upon government with an evangelical fervor that is reminiscent of the Childrens' Crusades—only the religion they preach is more government.

As the years pass, more and more are elected to office. None has ever earned a dollar in the free market, none has had to meet a payroll. They know nothing but the bureaucracy itself. They believe in what they do and the causes they promote. They understand how elections are won and lost because they have worked their way up the ladder by participating in elections throughout their public careers. By the time they reach their thirties, they are politically sophisticated bureaucrats.

What, on the other hand, has happened to their counterparts in college, the kids who studied business or science or engineering? They gravitated into the free market and have struggled successfully in the other world where the taxes are paid and real goods and services are provided. By the time they reach thirty, they have a vested interest in their chosen careers and aren't about to run for public office. In the meantime, the smartest and best of the bureaucrats are succeeding in government and are positioning themselves to run for public office.

In the California Assembly, there are seventeen young legislators who have been elected over the past few years who came directly from the bureaucracy. Every year there are more and more of them. What we are acquiring is a growing passel of committed social reformers holding public office. The community fusses and fumes over the expanding control these liberal hot shots demand but as yet hasn't awakened to the political phenomena that's taking place *because* of the full time legislature. Few people are aware that the bureaucracy is training and electing its own kind. The rest of us aren't even in the ball game.

California is no better off because we established a full time legislature, in fact we would be smart to go back from whence we came. The quality of legislator was better, more widely-experienced and knowledgeable, about the taxpayer as well as the bureaucrat.

If you live in a state that's contemplating going to a full time legislature, just think of good ole California. With a little bit of hard work you can get an eighteen-billion-dollar legislature just like ours—one that's working full time to give you all the government you can swallow.

16

Ze Mooz

IT WAS A beautiful fall day at Sacramento Municipal Airport. The air was cool and sharp, the sky a rich blue, and all objects could be crisply seen. It was a great day to start on my moose-hunting trip to Canada.

At that time, I was a relatively new legislator. The old guard had condescended to open their inner social circle and had tendered an invitation for me to go hunting with them in Canada.

I was delighted. I thoroughly enjoy hunting, and I welcomed the opportunity to accompany the sages of the senate into the northern tules.

Right off the bat, I knew this hunt would be different. Usually, I become deeply involved in the planning of any trip with my hunting companions. Half the joy is in organizing the gear, talking, planning the trip, choosing the rations, debating over what weapons to bring, reloading ammo, planning the route of travel, checking the weight of the pack; all of these details are to be savored, discussed, and rethought, right up to the last moment. However, this was not the case in this instance.

Whenever I would ask about any detail of the trip, I would receive the same jovial reply, "Just bring a rifle and hunting clothes. Everything has already been taken care of." Soon I got the impression that further questions were unnecessary and unwanted. I dropped the subject.

I didn't know who was going or how much it would cost me. I had a hunch that some lobbyists would be along to take care of the minor details, such as transportation, food, lodging, and money.

The old-guard senators weren't known for expending their own loot, and there seemed to be plenty of lobbyists around to pick up the tab. I figured it was best to keep my mouth shut and wait—so I did.

On the appointed day I was the first to arrive. I was pleasantly surprised to see a couple of colleagues who had reputations for hunting (but not for the four-legged variety of animals). They didn't have much gear with them; most carried heavy jackets, small suitcases, and rifles. Several didn't have weapons of any type. I felt sort of stupid next to my mound of gear.

I was loaded for anything. I had a 30.06 Remington with a four-power Bushnell scope, a 30-30 Winchester, a Browning 12-gauge shotgun, a .357-Magnum sidearm, and enough ammunition to quell an uprising of the natives. I had extra foul-weather apparel and survival equipment.

Before long, we were all assembled. It was quite a large crowd. We hadn't long to wait. A twin-engine turbo jet circled into the pattern and was soon taxiing over to where we were all assembled.

It was a large corporate executive jet. There were no company markings on the plane, but once I poked my head inside, I knew it wasn't for packing peons. The interior was all mahogany paneling with posh, soft, brown leather couches and swivel chairs. I felt I was in the office of a corporate president instead of in an airplane.

As we entered, we were greeted by a gentleman I had seen before but had never met. A pleasant chap, he looked and acted like a senior vice president—cordial, gracious and dapper. I was sure he was a lobbyist, but for whom I wasn't sure.

The pilot and copilot helped load all our gear into the baggage compartment. After we were all comfortably ensconced in our leather lounge chairs, complete with seat belts, we were off into the blue skies, headed for some unknown spot in Canada.

This was traveling in style. I thought I might as well enjoy it, because I knew it had to get rugged as soon as we arrived. Packing in, horses, saddle sores, riding to some distant pack station deep in the wilderness—I was sure all of this was yet to come. In fact, I welcomed it. But in the interim, if I had to travel to the far north, what a way to go!

As soon as we were in level flight, our Dapper Dan host cheerfully asked, "Anybody want something from the bar?" There was no bar in evidence. One of the senators asked for a Bloody Mary. His request was followed by others. Our host walked over to an immense, custom-built cabinet attached to the wall and opened the top. Underneath were a sink and glasses. He stooped over and opened the doors on enough liquor to inebriate an army.

"Who's for gin rummy?" asked one of the senior Nimrods. We all were.

Gin rummy was a favorite pastime of legislators and lobbyists. Many an evening has been happily wiled away over a game of cards when the legislature used to meet on a part-time basis. Then legislators usually left their families back in the district. The sessions were short, and a legislator wasn't away from his family except for three or four nights a week, and then for only four to five months at the most. In the evenings, gin rummy was the game to play. There were gin-rummy tournaments going all the time. In Sacramento the game is also known as "Bakersfield."

Most of the men on board ordered Bloody Marys. I opted for coffee. Small tables were secreted within the paneled walls and by swiveling about in the chairs and shifting the couches, excellent and comfortable provisions were made for playing "Bakersfield."

A gourmet buffet was being prepared by our host, complete with breads, cheeses, nuts, sliced meats, relishes, etc.

We traveled over California, Oregon, Washington, and Canada, drinking, eating, laughing, joking, and playing cards. In no time, we were all deeply engrossed in the card game and playing for a half a cent a point. Being competitive, I soon lost track of time and location. The plane was nearly on the ground when we put up the cards. The games were not completed, and so we stuffed our card hands into our pockets, intent on resuming the game later.

I hadn't the foggiest idea where we were. I asked and found out we were in "Prince" something or other. Canadians have a propensity to name many of their towns after some prince—Prince George, Prince Albert, Prince Clyde, Prince Gomez, etc. Unless you know one prince from another, you don't know where you are, even when you are told.

We were hustled into a bus and carted down to the river where several large pontoon planes awaited us. "Now, I thought, this is more like it. Now we are on our way into the real primitive backcountry of Canada."

We were soon flying over a sea of pine trees interrupted by an occasional lake or meadow. We were definitely on our way into the rugged backcountry. After almost an hour's flight, we were over a hundred miles deep into the Canadian wilderness. On the horizon loomed a huge blue lake, icy cold, lovely, and lonely.

We circled an island in the middle of the lake. The plane banked into a tight turn, throttled back, descended, and touched down. We taxied to a dock where two Indians awaited.

The pilot unloaded us and the plane was gone as quickly as it had arrived. The wind was crisply blowing across the lake. Small whitecaps could be seen on the windward side of the small island. As I stood on the wooden dock, looking over the lake, civilization seemed a million miles away.

The cold fall wind cut through the light jacket I was wearing, gently stinging my skin. The air carried the fragrance of pine and clean water. "This is the life," I said to myself. I turned and followed the rest of the body through the pine trees toward some buildings.

As we came closer, I became more and more awestruck. The log buildings were large and extremely well constructed. The logs had been debarked and the wood was varnished. Everything was trim, manicured, and posh. The place reeked of exclusivity.

We climbed the varnished wood staircase onto a large deck that surrounded the main building. The inside was varnished pine paneling with large bay windows, through which one could look out onto the lake. The furniture was hardwood and red leather. The dining room was large enough to accommodate three parties our size.

"Where's the bar?" asked someone. As if by magic, a neatly dressed Indian woman appeared.

"What do you wish to drink, sir?" she asked.

"Who's got the cards?" asked someone. Before we even unpacked, the card game was in full force. But there were still two hours of light left, and I wanted to look around.

An Indian bellhop escorted me to my varnished log cabin. My backwoods tepee had two bedrooms and a large area complete with kitchen, shower, white sheets, blankets, electricity, automatic heaters—a veritable Conrad Hilton North.

I unpacked my rod and fished along the shore for an hour or so—no luck. At dark I wandered back to the main lodge.

The card game was going full blast. The smoke was thick. The smell of booze permeated the air. The game paused while dinner was served. We had a menu and a choice of main courses and fine wines. We had to rough it somewhat—there were no oysters or lobster. Salmon, however, and trout dishes were offered, and the meal was excellent. After dinner the card game resumed.

"When do we go hunting?" I asked. "Those who want to hunt see the lodge manager tomorrow morning at sunup," was the response.

At dawn, only five of us gathered in the main lodge to

receive our hunting instructions. The lodge manager was organizing the day's hunt with our guides. We were paired up and assigned to an Indian guide. Since there were only five of us, I got a guide all to myself. I lucked out. I was assigned to the chief of the local tribe. His name was Pierre, no less. Hot dog! I was sure I had moose meat already in the freezer. With an Indian chief named Pierre, how could I miss? Pierre looked and sounded the part. The chief was one of the silent type, complete with folded arms, ughs and grunts.

When he finally spoke, I knew I had a trophy rack for my den wall. "Zenator, lez go down to ze boat and hunt ze mooz."

I eagerly followed Pierre down to the dock. The cold morning wind was exhilarating. The anticipation of the hunt, with my trusty guide, warmed me through and through. At the dock there was no rustic canoe awaiting. Instead, there was a sixteen-foot power launch, complete with cabin. Pierre started the engine and we were off across the lake.

I anticipated that once we reached the mainland, we would dock the boat and begin to hunt in earnest. The trip across the lake took twenty-five minutes. Instead of stopping, Pierre headed up the river that fed the lake. We were passed by a few Indians in power boats heading in the other direction. Before long, we chugged by a small Indian village. Pierre pointed. "Zenator, zat is my home!" A number of motorboats, adorned with Mercury engines, were docked at the river's edge—not a canoe or a tepee or a totem pole in sight, but square, wooden shacks, roofed with composition shingles. Barefoot, runny-nosed children, and barking dogs abounded.

We proceeded to chug upriver. After about an hour, I asked, "Pierre, when are we going to hunt?"

"We hunt now!" he responded.

"Are we going to pull ashore here?" I asked.

"No, we hunt from ze boat. See mooz along river. Shoot ze mooz from ze boat."

I was shocked. Some hunt! Cruising comfortably along the

river, sitting on my derriere, hoping to surprise some moose grazing along the swampy edge of the river. Fortunately, we saw nothing but beautiful scenery.

After a while, I suggested we fish, instead. Believe it or not, that turned out to be a bummer also. The river was teeming with lethargic, spawning salmon, and we were constantly hooking them accidentally in the side. The poor souls were on their last legs and, if caught, were worthless to eat.

We headed back to the lodge earlier than I had anticipated. Oh, well, I said to myself, we still have three days to go. Things will be looking up.

When I arrived back at the lodge, the card game was in full swing. The lodge was full of smoke and the smell of booze. No one even looked up to wave.

I asked the manager if I could hunt on foot the following day. "No problem," was the response. The next morning a plane awaited Pierre and me at the dock. We were whisked into the air and within fifteen minutes were deposited on the shore of a small lake deep within the forest. We arranged to meet the plane slightly before dark at the same spot. The plane took off, and Pierre and I were alone, deep in the wilds of Canada.

The terrain was deeply timbered. The area most likely to hold the moose was the marshy tributaries on the other end of the lake. We would have the difficult job of working our way around the lake to the far shore through the dense timber. Hardship or not, at least I felt as if I were hunting! It started to drizzle and the rain was cold.

I soon began to have big doubts about the success of our hunt. Pierre, my trusty Indian guide, kept falling down and tripping over logs, rocks, and twigs. I had never seen such a clumsy Indian. He was noisy, to boot. I have never been known for my silent stalking ability, but compared to Pierre, I was the master. He made noise leaning up against a tree. My worst fears were confirmed when, later in the day, I had to help him start a fire. Pierre was a country-club Indian guide. I doubt that he had many requests to leave the comforts of the power-boat and stomp his way through the wilderness. Pierre didn't look too happy about having to guide this crazy paleface.

After Pierre had fallen from atop a large rock, ricocheted off a log, and finally come to rest in a batch of blackberry bushes, I couldn't help thinking that I had better start paying attention to where we were. This turkey guide could get us both lost! I could tell that Pierre wanted to go back and wait for the plane, but I was determined to continue hunting.

We finally worked our way around the lake to its head-waters. We spotted a cow contentedly grazing among the lily pads; however, no bull moose was in sight.

Pierre was, by this time, mumbling French-English-Indian four-letter adjectives under his breath—"Sacre bleu," "Got tam!" We stumbled and sloshed our way around the lake. We crashed through a stand of lodgepole pine, tripped through some quaking aspens, and suddenly found ourselves staring at a cow moose belly-deep in lily pads some hundred yards before us.

Cows weren't in season, and I had no intention of shooting one, anyway. I wanted a bull moose and, besides, removing a drowned cow from four and a half feet of water is no joy—and with Pierre along, the job seemed doubly onerous.

"Well, Pierre," I whispered, "what should we do now?"

"Zenator, we wait."

"Why?"

"Maybe," he smiled knowingly, "just maybe, ze cow is in ze mood for love and ze big bull will come along. Zen we shoot ze papa mooz!"

We hunkered down behind some bushes and waited and waited. The cow kept munching on lily pads and underwater grass. The drizzling rain had by this time found its way into every corner of my apparel. We tried to keep as quiet as we could, but any silence we accomplished by nonmovement was overcome by Pierre's chattering teeth.

We watched the cow consume an enormous amount of food

before Pierre turned to me and with teeth chattering said, "Zenator, maybe zis cow is not ready for ze love." His lips were blue. Pierre was a game Indian, but one cold Canadian Canuck.

"Pierre," I said, "let's head back to where the plane is to pick us up and fix a bite to eat." He was obviously pleased. He grunted approval and commenced to crash his way back.

On arrival, Pierre fumbled around, unsuccessfully trying to start a fire. I rummaged around and found some pitch bark, and we soon had a roaring fire. Together, we warmed ourselves until the plane arrived.

We were still cold and numb when we arrived back at the main lodge. As I walked by, the card game was in full force. The dining room was again filled with the smell of booze and cigar smoke. Again, I was hardly noticed.

The next morning Pierre and I were back in the boat, cruising up the river, looking for ze mooz. By this time Pierre and I had become friends. We had a few things in common. He was chief of his tribe–elected, no less. I was the elected leader of the nineteenth-district tribe of California. It seems that amongst Pierre's constituency, the dude who can get the best deals for the tribe from the Canadian government is the ranking Indian. Pierre was a diplomat, and his tribe elected him chief because of it. What irony! I had traveled thousands of miles to get stuck with a politician as my guide.

Pierre was also a compassionate man. He observed that my desire to hunt the moose was real. As our friendship grew, he became more committed to finding me a bull "mooz."

This day was also a total loss. As darkness fell, Pierre knew there was only one more day left to hunt.

"Zenator," he blurted, "you will not shoot ze mooz unless you are ze first man on ze river in ze morning. We cannot leave ze lodge in ze middle of ze lake and get to ze river before my tribe has already shot ze mooz."

It suddenly dawned on me. All of those Indian boats we had been passing had already been up the river for "ze mooz."

And any white face that saw a moose to shoot at was fortunate indeed. The Indians from Pierre's village had picked the river clean.

Pierre continued, "Zenator, why don't we stay at my cousin's cabin on ze river and get out on ze river an shoot ze mooz firs thing dawn come."

I thought about my colleagues back at the lodge and wondered what they would do if Pierre and I didn't show up for dinner. But I assumed they would conclude we were all right. It was a correct assumption. They didn't stop shuffling the cards long enough to check.

We chugged upriver for what seemed to be hours. It was pitch black when we spotted the lights of Pierre's cousin's cabin. The lamplights of the house silhouetted Pierre's cousin and his family as we trudged up from the dock.

"Hallo, Pierre," shouted Pierre. "It is I, Pierre!"

Pierre's cousin, Pierre, had constructed a small, bare wooden shack with a galvanized roof next to his home. Two single bunk beds were in the corners, and a small wood stove leaned against the wall. The rent was five bucks. After twelve hours in the boat, it looked like the Waldorf-Astoria. We purchased two cans of beans and a half loaf of bread from Cousin Pierre. He threw in a cup of coffee grounds, gratis. We warmed the beans in the cans, made coffee on the top of the wood stove, and feasted.

Pierre's cousin joined us in conversation. A few moments later, two of his children entered the room. Both stood silently and expressionless before us until, minutes later, their papa recognized their presence. "What you want, huh?" asked Cousin Pierre.

The older one was about four and a half years old. The younger was about three. The younger had a dirty towel over his shoulders; both wore only dungarees without shirts or shoes. It was early fall and the evening was drizzly cold, but the cold didn't seem to bother them. Both had runny noses.

"Papa," responded the older, "Pierre has a hook stuck in his back." (Believe it or not, the younger's name was Pierre also.) Until that time, I had heard three Indian names, and they were all Pierre.

"Ugh," grunted Cousin Pierre. "Come here and let papa see." The two walked toward their father and stood before him.

Cousin Pierre and Chief Pierre were sitting next to each other on a bench. I was in a chair next to them. The older boy turned little Pierre around and removed the towel. Deeply embedded in his skin was a large treble hook attached to a large four-inch fishing plug. Two of the barbs were completely under the skin. The father didn't say a word, but grunted matter-of-factly. He reached out and grasped the plug and jiggled it a few times. The kid didn't bat an eye.

"Hey, dot's in real goot," offered Chief Pierre.

"Ugh," replied Cousin Pierre. He jiggled the hook once again, testing how deep it had embedded itself into his son's back.

Once again the Indian boy remained silent.

I am the father of three children, and if any one of them had a treble hook stuck in his back, the screams would be recorded on the world's seismographs while his mother demanded treatment at the Mayo Clinic. Here this kid stood stone-still while his father played around with the hooks.

It's true, I thought to myself, Indians are braver and never cry. I was deeply impressed with the stoic behavior of the entire family.

"Hey," advised Chief Pierre, "you better push ze hooks through ze skin and file off ze barbs, zen pull it out."

The father stood up and took his small son by the hand and led him out of our shack to their cabin. I never did find out how the hooks were extracted. I heard no cries coming from the cabin.

The next morning Pierre and I had the first boat on the river. Still no luck. I did see one heck of a lot of Indians in power-boats cruising up and down the river at dawn's early light.

After another unsuccessful day we headed back to the lodge. We stopped off on the way so Pierre could see Cousin

Pierre about some private matter. I saw little Pierre tightly clutching a wiggling kitten to his chest. Next to him was an overturned fishing boat on the beach. Little Pierre tripped and dropped the kitten, which immediately sought refuge under the boat. The lad let out a scream that would have deafened a bull moose. Tears streamed down his face as he ran, crying, into the arms of an older sister.

I was dumbstruck. No tears with a treble hook stuck in his back, but a flood of anguish over the temporary loss of a kitten. Kids are kids the world over.

The sun had settled as we made it back to the island lodge. I bade a fond adieu to Pierre, retired to my cottage, showered, and changed into clean clothes. I hadn't eaten since the night before and was starved.

The lounge was filled with smoke, and drinks adorned the card tables. The game was still in full swing.

The trip back was a repeat of the trip up. Once the plane was off the ground, the bar opened and we played cards all the way back.

As we departed the plane in Sacramento, one of my colleagues, who had never left the lodge, stretched and yawned. "Bill, it's great therapy to go into the great outdoors to relax. I feel like a million bucks. It's just wonderful what a hunting trip can do for a man!"

He really meant it. Hard as it is to believe, I still don't know who the host was. What meager contributions I made to the trip couldn't have covered all of the expenses.

Trips like that are a thing of the past. A hopperful of new laws have been passed to restrict California lobbyists from buying a legislator a hot dog without reporting it, much less a hunting trip to Canada. However, special interests will find, and have found, other ways to snuggle up to their favorite solons. Let's face it. What flimflam man could pass up a mark with an eighteen-billion-dollar bankroll?

17

Ancient Origins of Lobbying

ANCIENT MYTHOLOGY holds that lobbying came about when primordial man discovered the correlation between working and eating. Work wasn't well received by some; in fact, a sizable segment of society tried to avoid it entirely. This created an unpleasant problem, hunger pangs. Resorting to work, then, became the primary mode of relieving these gastric anxieties.

The industrious reconciled themselves to this cruel fact of life and proceeded to toil, but those who had a psychological block against disturbing the body metabolism set about coveting the products of the industrious.

Stealing was a chancy endeavor, often quite unprofitable, since the industrious resisted. So the plunderers banded together in order to gang up on the productive members of society and pick them off one by one. And so it was for many, many years. In the interest of historical accuracy, it should be noted that the system tended to become inoperative when the society ran out of producers.

One day, according to the legend, a group of hard-working serfs in the tiny kingdom of Welfaria held a great meeting to which all of the great philosophers and teachers were invited. The serfs of Welfaria were not noted as a clever people, but their reputation as industrious workers was known to all. Because of this, they were particularly hard hit by the thievery system. The more they produced, the more frequent and vicious the raids.

On the day of the great meeting, the serfs presented their case to the wise members of the panel. When they had completed their testimony, the serfs listened eagerly as the professors began to speak.

"Considering the socioeconomic nature of the problem . . . ," began one.

"Graphs! We need graphs!" shouted another as he began rummaging through his briefcase.

"Hypothetically speaking . . . ," began a third. When the meeting broke up for lunch, the bewildered serfs wandered out of the room thoroughly confused.

"I didn't understand one word they said," complained one of the productive Welfarians. "Why don't we just go in there after lunch, tell them our problem in simple terms, present a simple solution, and just ask those eggheads if they agree? If they do, then that's all there is to it." The others concurred, and so back they went to the meeting.

When the afternoon session convened, the leader of the serfs rose awkwardly to his feet and began to speak. "Fellow Welfarians, we work hard, but to no avail. All that we produce is taken away from us by those roving bands of marauders. Well, enough is enough!"

"Yeah!" came the chorus of affirmation from the gallery.

"It's time to act," he continued. "I propose that we set up a government with a king. The king will have the power to provide police to protect our citizens from thieves and an army to protect us from foreign invaders. Furthermore, the king would hear disputes that arise among our citizens and dispense justice in a peaceful fashion—a system I believe to be far better than the current practice of bashing in one another's heads!

"In conclusion," he said as he turned toward the panel of professors, "we work but we do not eat. I ask you, is this not a futile system?"

The professors looked at one another, shrugging their shoulders, and then replied matter of factly, "Of course, it's a feudal system!"

With that, the serfs rushed out of the room to select a king, leaving the academicians scratching their heads.

All went well under the new king, and the tiny kingdom of Welfaria prospered. Needless to say, crime soon became a depressed industry. One day the leader of the crooks addressed his fellow felons. "I tink we've been going about dis ting all wrong, fellas. We've been getting our skulls dented and our bodies stretched all out of shape for no good reason. Gentlemen, dere has got to be a better way.

"We gotta get organized," he added. "We'll hire a fancy P.R. man and call ourselves 'Welfarians Advocating No-Toil Subsidies' (WANTS). We send our representatives to take da king to lunch, see. Buy him a coupla drinks, if youse knows what I mean. After all, we're economically disadvantaged, aren't we? Our educational opportunities were retarded, weren't they? I mean, who is more socially maladjusted than us, right?"

"Right," replied his cohorts. "We want our fair share!"

So WANTS hired an agreeable old gentleman named Lobbius to plead its case before the king. Unlike the slovenly group of scoundrels whom he represented, Lobbius was a pleasant, well-dressed man noted for his witty conversation and pleasing personality. WANTS correctly assumed that the king was a kindly, benevolent old soul who wanted nothing more than to be popular among his subjects. Surely, the king would see the logic of no-toil subsidies. Instead of stealing a lot from a few, through the subsidy program the crooks would steal a little from everybody.

And so Lobbius set off for the king's castle, complete with expense account and box seats at the weekly joust. The first legislative advocate was born.

The king's treasury consisted of taxes collected from all of the industrious members of the kingdom of Welfaria. Obviously, there was no gold in the coffers from those who didn't work. Just as one can't squeeze blood from a turnip, one can't squeeze taxes from a nonproducer.

The taxes were paid to the king to keep the robbers, thieves, and roving bands of looters at a minimum.

WANTS' silver-tongued advocate met little opposition. It wasn't long before he had asked the king out to lunch and convinced His Majesty of the merit of WANTS' wants. The king went along with the idea, although he insisted upon setting up a pilot project first to see if it would work. A bureau was set up to handle the pilot project. And so it was that soon after the arrival of the first legislative advocate, the first subsidy was born.

Glowing reports were submitted to the king by the administrators (who liked their jobs). "The pilot project is a success," they all agreed. So, hearing nothing but good, the kindly king expanded the program each year.

Then the industrious noticed an appreciable rise in their taxes.

"What goes on?" they asked. "Where are all of our hard-earned tax dollars going? We better send a representative down to the castle to find out."

They did, and he did.

"The king has gone bananas," reported their representative. "He has been sold a bill of goods by a group called WANTS. They have convinced the king to fork over some of our tax dollars. We had better form an organization."

They agreed and formed the "Group of Toiling Serfs" (GOTS). They also sent a full-time representative to the king's court to keep an eye out for GOTS' gots.

Now a different kind of lobbyist loomed on the horizon, one who represented the GOTS against the WANTS. That's the way it has been ever since. Those who got and those who want and those who represent both groups in the legislative halls of the world.

Over the years, lobbying has developed into a very sophisticated business, but the basic reason for the existence of the profession—*to use the power of government to force the public to do that which it refuses to do voluntarily*—remains the same.

The well-meaning king was the real culprit. He forgot his job description—protecting the public from being unlawfully coerced and robbed. When the king accepted the notion that he had the "right" to take tax dollars collected for the maintenance of public order and the administration of justice and dispense them as he saw fit, he made the first mistake. The government was originally set up to protect the citizens from robbers. Now the government had become an unwitting accomplice to the crime of plunder, "legalized" by the king's action. The only difference was that all the taxpayers lost a little instead of a few losing a lot.

The principle of legalized plunder is still with us today, alive and prospering. Instead of a king, we have a legislature—a covey of kings—sipping martinis and trying to satisfy all the wants.

"Ignorance ain't our problem, it's all that we know that ain't true."

—WILL ROGERS

18

The Majority Elects?

AMERICANS SUPPOSEDLY know about politics since we all can be involved in the elective process. But a lot that we know about politics is a lot of nonsense.

In a democracy we "know" the majority elects. Right? Wrong! Majorities rarely, if ever, elect.

In a democracy most politicians are inevitably influenced by public opinion. Right? Wrong again.

If you believe majorities elect and public opinion usually affects how most politicians vote, then you are buying two false assumptions, assumptions that can seriously affect your ability to be politically effective.

First, we need properly to understand that the political axioms which tell us that "majorities elect" and that "public opinion influences the legislature" are half-truths, at best.

Turning to the first of these half-truths, it can be safely stated that if we waited for majorities to elect, most of our legislative chambers would be empty. Obviously, only those who register can vote (or so we are told). This eliminates a sizable portion of the eligible voters at the very start. In fact, the very term "eligible voter" tells us that there are those who are ineligible to vote. Among these are persons disfranchised

112

for reason of age, mental deficiency, or insufficient length of residency.

In most states, a potential voter must register by party affiliation. Since the contest almost inevitably comes down to Democrat versus Republican, those who register as "independent" or who "decline to state" have little or nothing to say in the primary elections. To have a meaningful voice, these independent and uncommitted voters must then choose between the two candidates fielded by the very political parties they have chosen not to join. Since sizable numbers of voters do just that, these political eunuchs are eliminated from the primary selection process from which the eventual winner will emerge.

I can understand why a person would be hesitant to register either Republican or Democrat—it's often like choosing between two social diseases. Registering in either party carries with it all of the germs associated with the body and choosing one or the other tends to make a lot of people break out in a rash.

Not all of those who register to vote bother to exercise that privilege in the all-important primaries when the candidates are selected. Not uncommon is it to see less than fifty percent of the registered voters turn out in a primary election. Needless to say, an unused franchise is little better than no franchise at all.

A vote delivers the power of the state into the hands of the elected official. A nonvote simply transfers the decision as to who shall hold this power into the hands of those who do vote. Clearly, then, the power of government condenses into the hands of those who understand the actual dynamics of this process of "majority rule."

At this point, another factor comes into play—gerrymandering. Most political district lines are established by the party in power. This is usually accomplished by arranging the district lines in such a manner as to give overwhelming majorities to the opposition party in a few select districts while creating a larger number of districts with comfortable majorities for one's own party.

Party-registration imbalance significantly diminishes the chances of victory for the minority party in a district. This results in a lessening ability of the minority party to attract good candidates since the chances of ultimate victory are slight. A candidate with little chance of victory has even a smaller chance of attracting the necessary financial support. Money creates winners and winners attract money. This cycle is in large part created and sustained by the gerrymandering system. Seldom, if ever, does redistricting result in a large number of districts in which the party affiliation of the eventual winner is in doubt.

Accordingly, while the minority party attracts poor candidates (in both senses of the word), the majority party has a host of hopefuls to choose from. Since the primary nominee is likely to emerge as the eventual winner, the real contest for the office is therefore waged in the primary election, months before the independents and decline-to-state voters can even cast their ballots.

This process of condensing political power goes a step further. Since the majority-party primary is usually crowded with a number of hopefuls, the primary winner is quite often nominated with a plurality of twenty-five percent, or even less. I know of one district that had a population of 525,000 persons. About 400,000 could have qualified to vote, but only 225,000 bothered to register. In the primary slightly more than fifty percent of those registered turned out at the polls to vote—about 120,000 people altogether. The minority party garnered 50,000 votes of that total, split between two lackluster candidates. The majority party had eight candidates, of whom five were strong contenders. The remaining 70,000 votes were split among these eight candidates, and the victor won with 16,000. In the general election this candidate easily defeated the minority-party nominee because all of the advantages—money, workers, lopsided party registration— were on his side.

Majority? Those 16,000 votes are hardly a majority. Let's look at it again:

Total population	525,000
Qualified to register	400,000
Actually registered	225,000
Total primary vote	120,000
Majority-party primary vote	70,000
Winning plurality	16,000

Surprisingly, the winning candidate defeated his nearest rival by 6,000 votes in the primary and his victory was regarded as a landslide. Once in office, the advantages of incumbency made the task of dislodging him virtually impossible. This particular individual was very public-relations oriented and used the platform which his office provided to promote his philosophy. His column appears regularly in dozens of newspapers and his radio spots are aired statewide. He owns not a single newspaper, not one radio or television station, but he uses all of these outlets to promote his philosophy, which, incidentally, the editorial boards of most of the media outlets do not support.

The question, then, is, *Who constitutes his constituency—* the 525,000 who reside in his district or the 16,000 who elected him? Or those who supplied him with the political know-how and the financial wherewithal to put those 16,000 votes together and win the election? Of course, once in office the incumbent can do practically anything he jolly well pleases as long as he doesn't land in jail or make a complete fool of himself. Recent events might convince us that even these last two political blunders are not sufficient to ensure defeat, providing the incumbent has gone through at least the perfunctory motions of the office.

Once ensconced in that leather chair, many politicians avail themselves of the benefactions of the public through "communication with the people." It is this dedication to the public's right to know which, no doubt, is responsible for those traveling road-show committee hearings which are frequently scheduled in the committee chairman's district just prior to election day. And, of course, no discussion of incumbency would be complete without a passing reference to those "non-partisan" legislative newsletters mailed at public expense. So much for the notion that majorities elect.

The second half-truth is that public opinion influences the legislature. While it is true that public opinion does have an influence, it is not the kind that one might think. Aside from providing an indication of what might be safely inserted into a speech at a local chamber of commerce meeting, public opin-ion and public-opinion polls have little effect on many politi-cians.

Political office has been a major platform for the dissemina-tion of radical ideas. A group of philosophical brethren can succeed in achieving public office by understanding the dynamics of the condensation of political power. Once there, they "hire their own kind and elect others of like mind." In time, with tax dollars, committees, commissions, agencies, and bureaus are created and staffed with kindred spirits. Stacked committees, aided by ideologically committed con-sultants, listen to unsubstantiated testimony from friendly witnesses who often have a direct, vested interest in the dispo-sition of the legislation under consideration. Based upon the phony committee "hearings," legislation is introduced and passed into law by legislators who, more times than not, are concerned more with who endorsed or opposed the bill than with what the bill will do if passed.

Public opinion? Seriously, do you really care what the Upper Nile Watusis think about urban renewal? Does your heart palpitate until the morning paper arrives and you can check the box scores of the Eastern Mongolian javelin-catching semifinals? Does your blood pressure rise and fall with the annual rainfall statistics from Malta? If you answered affirmatively, either your stockbroker is the last of the great mavericks or you should be awarded the Empathy of the Year Medallion.

On the other hand, if things which do not affect your life have little effect on you, then you are like many other Americans—and most politicians. The hard facts are, most people do not even know their representative's name, much less whether his votes on controversial legislation matched prevailing public opinion. To make matters worse, most legislators know that.

Public opinion is an ethereal, intangible commodity. What's big stuff one day is forgotten tomorrow. Legislators know that too. Public opinion has no force unless harnessed and translated into effective action.

Politicians fear not public opinion, but those individuals or organizations which are capable of harnessing that force into political action. I stress political because unless it is political, it has no meaning in the political realm.

Perhaps an example might best illustrate the point. Let us say that the folks in North County are upset over increased property tax bills. Everybody is griping and complaining. Big deal.

Finally, someone lands upon the bright idea to "do something." "Let's get together and have a rally at the park." A few citizens print signs and posters, and the following Saturday afternoon the park is jampacked with North County taxpayers. Speeches are delivered, but nothing new is presented because each speaker is saying what everyone knows already.

"The taxes are too high . . . downright oppressive!" says one.

"Yeah," responds the crowd.

More speeches, more applause from the crowd, and everyone goes home, happy because "action" was taken. Big deal.

Perhaps the local legislator sent a telegram to the gathering expressing his support. More likely he ignored the gathering altogether. The following week a second rally is held and 400 property taxpayers sign a petition which is then sent to the legislator. A polite letter is received in response to the petition.

It expresses "concern" and promises to "study the matter thoroughly." North County public opinion is virtually unanimous. But again, nothing happens. Why?

The problem is that the people of North County think their opinions are important to their elected representatives. They are confused and disillusioned when their protests bring no action. Taxes are still oppressive and climbing steadily. Those who understand the political process, however, realize that public opinion is not always a big deal.

This particular legislator has ignored the North County constituents for several reasons. First among them, North County residents are notorious for not registering to vote. As far as the elected official is concerned, their opinions rank in importance somewhere between the views of Upper Segurabli aborigines on the decline and fall of the Roman Empire, and the pronouncements of an Arab at a meeting of the Jewish Defense League. If North County residents cannot affect the legislator's reelection chances, then their opinions simply don't count.

Meanwhile, the residents of South County have organized a committee to promote the building of new parks, subsidized by the state, of course. The South County Association is run by activists, however, who conduct yearly registration drives and precinct-level campaigns to get out the vote. When election time rolls around, they are Johnny-on-the-spot to help their friend in the legislature with money and manpower.

Although constituting a minority of the total population, they constitute a sizable bloc of activist voters. Their representatives lobby the legislators. And so, knowing how to make the right squeaks, they are first in line to get the legislative oil. Stated another way, they get their backs scratched, with somebody else's "scratch."

I suppose that there are some who would prefer to remain in ignorance of the politics of condensation and the half-truths of majority rule and public opinion. Indeed, the failure to recognize these principles in action may serve to explain the failure of an American majority—a majority that calls itself conservative, according to the polls, but that appears incapable of effecting political action consistent with its principles.

Whether that majority is or is not "conservative" in a philosophical sense is largely immaterial, actually. The political and economic freedoms which are inherent in the American system and which we seek to "conserve" are made neither valid nor moral by sheer force of numbers. Shall a majority vote affirming that black is white make it so? No, but that does not prevent such an affirmation from becoming public policy.

While the problem at hand is political, the inability of responsible people to stem the tide of social, political, economic, and theological irresponsibility is largely a philosophical problem. Entire movements are built upon imbecilic predictions of impending doom. There are some who don't even wish to succeed, because to do so would disprove their predisposed notions of the ultimacy of evil in this world. Having turned their backs on God's promise of the triumph of justice and righteousness, they are resigned to sulking about, muttering Chicken Littleisms, and bemoaning the lack of light in the world while standing knee-deep in matches.

Do the facts that majorities don't elect and that public opinion isn't the dominant factor in how solons vote depress you? It does some people. Some folks believe these are motherhood concepts and to prove them inaccurate is tantamount to accusing Snow White of being a Hollywood hooker.

There is no big deal in majorities—certainly, "majority" cannot be equated with "morality." Pluralities have never been a guarantee of right. Public opinion is inevitably a condensation of collective ignorance as well as knowledge. The fact that public opinion is no guideline to public morality is no sin.

Facts are facts, nonetheless. Accurate information is always a tool. If majorities don't elect, then shouldn't we rejoice and become part of the minority that does? If public opinion doesn't affect how a legislator votes, then find out what does, and do it.

19

The Pot Shoot

THERE IS a little ham in every politician. In fact, the process of becoming a politician weeds out those who don't like to appear on a public platform.

I served eight years in the California Senate when Ronald Reagan was governor and heard many a gripe about actors becoming politicians, usually from those who would upstage their grandmothers at family reunions. Politicians seek recognition. In fact, they often demand it.

Recently, a western governor was incensed when at a press luncheon the audience did not rise to its feet when he entered the room. He commented on it loudly enough so that those within the first five rows could hear. Appropriately, the local press fried his egotistical hide.

Why are so many "dignitaries" introduced at political events?

Why? Because an astute master of ceremonies knows that it is better to introduce everybody in the audience than spend weeks unruffling political feathers. A person has to have a bit of an ego even to consider politics. Those who loudly deny that ego plays any part in their decision to enter politics and who loudly proclaim that their sole motivation is to serve the people are fooling no one but themselves. To believe one can serve and then to submit one's self to the rigors of campaigning in competition with others is all the affirmation needed to establish egotism. To illustrate the point, we need look only at the case of a past California attorney general.

The attorney general of California is responsible for the enforcement of our narcotic laws. There is a department in his office that works full time attempting to contain the illegal flow of drugs in California. It was a good law-enforcement department, and it often seized sizable quantities of contraband. The department policy was to destroy the drugs by burning in an unceremonial but, nevertheless, effective fashion.

On one occasion, the department had been unusually successful, seizing a sizable shipment of marijuana. One of the bright young deputy attorneys landed upon a bright idea and, according to procedure, shared his inspiration with the state's attorney general. The conversation must have gone something like this. "Chief, don't you think you are wasting a great opportunity to show the public the effectiveness of our Narcotics Division and your masterful handling of the attorney general's office?

"How so?"

"Chief, look at all that pot we picked up—all those bennies, reds, uppers, downers, hash, coke, and so on. It all goes up in flames without the public ever knowing the volume of the work our office handles. We should be more graphic, more demonstrative mediawise in our disposal of a stash like this."

"What do you suggest?" questioned the now attentive attorney general.

"Chief," said the bright deputy, "why don't we load it all on a barge and take it out past the San Francisco Golden Gate Bridge and dump it into the ocean? We can have launches accompanying us with members of the media to witness this event."

"Do you think the media would be interested?" inquired the attorney general.

"Interested? Does C. B. De Mille love pyramids? Does Bambi love the forest? Does a bear eat berries? Chief, they will *love* it! And, more important, so will the public."

"The public?" queried the chief.

"Of course! They are crying for action against narcotics.

This will show them what a fine job you are doing." The attorney general agreed. It would be heartless for him to deprive the public of its right to know just what a simply marvelous job his administration was doing.

On the appointed day, a barge was loaded to the hilt with bundles of marijuana, as well as hundreds of bottles and vials full of reds and yellows, enough to send the most discriminating dopehead up, down, and sideways. Watchful guards, armed to the teeth with rifles and pistols, surrounded the area. Fully showcased was the awesome power of the attorney general's office.

Amidst dignified fanfare, the tug commenced to tow the barge out into the bay, through the Golden Gate, and out into the Pacific. The barge was surrounded with boats filled with reporters, TV cameramen, and the like. It was a smashing public-relations success—that is until they arrived at the appointed spot a few miles offshore.

At the command of the attorney general, the deputies and officers commenced to throw the bundles of narcotics into the ocean. Unfortunately, no one took into account the nature of marijuana. It is a woody substance and doesn't sink. By the time this fact was noticed, bundles and bundles of hash were bobbing along atop the water like so many brown corks in a bathtub. Then, suddenly, bottles, vials, and baggies began popping to the surface.

There was a brief moment of shock on the barge where the attorney general's forces were assembled. All the while, the TV cameras were grinding away at the bobbing bales of floating euphoria while radio reporters were giving on-the-spot descriptions of how the winds were carrying the stash into the San Francisco North Beach shore.

"Shoot 'em!" someone shouted. "Blast 'em, dagnabit!" The army of narcotic officers and guards opened fire on the bobbing targets of contraband. A hail of bullets rained down on the bottles and bales. Dignitaries dove for cover while the reporters and cameramen collapsed into a giggling, hysterical heap.

What Makes You Think We Read The Bills?

Despite the barrage, amounts of illegal drugs escaped to
float merrily toward shore. Within hours marijuana fiber dot-
ted the north area beaches, and bottles and baggies continued
to drift ashore for several weeks thereafter.

Suddenly, picnicking was in. Hundreds of youths could be
observed camping out on the beaches, sitting on soggy blankets in the pouring rain, peering through binoculars at the
incoming tide while munching on cold chicken.

In a few weeks the bonanza was over, but the poor attorney
general (now retired) never lived it down. While hyperactive
egos and politicians seem to go together, we must remember
that ego can act as a spice to the political soup we Americans
mix for ourselves, or that it, blended with the expanding,
arbitrary power bestowed upon American politicians, can produce a very dangerous combination—like fire and powder.
And that kind of mixture is no joke at all.

20

The God Demos

THE FLOOR of the legislature was looked upon as a verbal jousting field where gentlemen gathered for a duel of ideas. A field of honor, so to speak, where undue advantage was never taken of a weaker opponent, where chivalry lived among men of good will.

A man's word was his bond, and shame and disgrace were the lot of a legislator who would lie or break his word to a colleague.

Although this was never entirely achieved, it was at least attempted by many legislators. Honor did have its place. Today the illusive god Demos (god of the majority) rules the roost, as far as many legislators are concerned. To them, majority rule means moral rule.

Once that premise is accepted, it becomes moral to keep an opponent down, once he is there. It becomes right to do so, to make sure the ideas of one's opposition aren't taught in the public schools, to exclude their opinions when holding committee hearings, to hire consultants who agree only with one side, and to make new laws that guarantee continuation of one's philosophy in government.

This should surprise no one. These individuals are doing nothing more than they deem necessary to perpetuate the status quo. If one has the votes, it's moral. That is the prevailing standard of the day—might makes right. (The only surprise is that those who actually work to maintain the status quo are called liberals, whereas their philosophical opponents are called, ironically, conservatives.)

Since the statist mentality permeates and controls the Democratic Party apparatus, statist-quo liberals know their percentages increase if they can register more Democrats. These men are well aware that as concerns the lower offices (state assembly and senate, as opposed to U.S. Congress, governor, and President), when in doubt, people usually vote the party in which they are registered.

Not too many years ago, a bill was introduced giving voters the right to register as late as a few days before election. For a variety of reasons, it was obvious that the bill favored the Democrats. (Obvious to me, at least.) It was carried by the Democratic caucus chairman. It was supported on the floor by members of the Democratic leadership and was obviously advantageous to them. The arguments made for the bill had little relevance to what the bill would do. The arguments were that the bill would give more rights to minority voters, open new avenues of citizen participation, bring increased citizen involvement within the mainstream of the political process, etc.

It registered more Democrats, pure and simple. If it registered more Republicans, would the Democratic leadership have introduced it? Hardly. When the vote was taken, the bill passed with no problem whatsoever because several Republican senators voted for it.

I was aghast! Why would a man in his right mind go out of his way to vote for a bill which obviously registered more of the opposition party in his district? I went over to an old-line Democratic senator and I said to him, "I can certainly understand why you have contempt for the Republicans. Wouldn't that bill give your party a distinct advantage?" "Of course, it would," he said. "Wouldn't that bill give you an opportunity to register more Democrats?"

"But, of course," he replied.

"Why, then, would a Republican vote for that particular bill?"

He smiled, looked me dead in the eye, and responded, "What do you expect if you've got clay for brains." I then walked over to one of the Republican senators who voted for the bill and repeated verbatim the conversation that had just taken place. The senator responded, "That's just one man's opinion."

"No," I said, "not one, that's two men's opinion!"

One of the tragedies of the legislative process is that within · the ranks of the parties we have people who are absolute Pollyannas. Some legislators have the capacity to believe anything and everything that is told to them. Why? Because they want to believe; because it would disturb them to believe that someone wasn't telling them the exact truth on every issue.

The particular senator in question eventually ceased to present a problem since the following year he was defeated (after serving only one term). The Democrats turned out the voters and, along with the newly registered Democrats, succeeded in defeating my colleague. His gullibility cost him his seat. I really don't feel sorry for him, because if you have "clay for brains," you don't deserve to stay in the legislature.

Although I disagree with these Democrats, I must at least give them credit for understanding the nature of government power and then using that power to advance their beliefs. I can also understand their contempt for the claybrains that inhabit our political halls—the perennial maidens who are deflowered with regularity.

Maybe childlike faith is a necessary ingredient for the survival of some legislators in the legislative process. These legislators display an inordinate degree of confidence in the honesty of their colleagues and witnesses before committees where one has only the word of a witness or colleague to go on as he describes the merits of the bill.

One assumes everyone tells the truth, but testimony is rarely given under oath, and witnesses can lie through their teeth before committees, with no fear of legal retribution. One assumes at his own risk that there is an unwritten rule that one's colleagues will always tell the truth when explaining a bill. I have a sneaking suspicion that this ethic is conveniently bent on occasion. Temporary amnesia is a legislative affliction.

One can accept as an article of legislative faith that everyone who sponsors legislation has the best interests of the public at heart. When teachers ask for more money to "upgrade the children's education," one mustn't think that eighty-five percent of that usually goes for teacher salary increases. One must somehow believe it is the children who benefit, not the teacher.

Whenever social workers ask for more money for their department, one mustn't believe that they are empire-building and using the welfare recipient as an excuse to do so. Whenever a special committee is set up to investigate this or that, one must believe that the purposes of the committee are 99 and 44/100 percent pure and that the committee chairman isn't using it as a platform to propagandize at the taxpayer's expense.

Whenever the stated intent is challenged, fellow legislators are horrified. Gadzooks! Are you questioning the INTEGRITY of the author? How could you? How uncouth to believe there could be an ulterior motive! How ungentlemanly to attribute anything but the purest of motives to the author! Legislators find it convenient to believe whatever they are told. If they don't question the integrity of their colleagues, then later their own integrity will presumably escape scrutiny. It's a neat little tradeoff.

There are unwritten social do's and don'ts in opposing legislation. It is taboo to question the author's stated intent, but it is perfectly permissible to argue the technical aspects of a bill. It is also permissible to argue the final impact of legislation but not if you imply that someone could get financially fat.

It is acceptable to be a fiscal conservative, although one is likely to be called a heartless tightwad for being such. One

may question the effectiveness of a project and say that the
legislation won't do what it is intended. That too is an acceptable argument. One may say that it isn't needed, that the law is
poorly drafted, and that there are other alternatives. All of
these are acceptable arguments but, it is indecorous to question
the *motives* of the proponents and imply that they are other
than stated.

Whenever a legislator goofs and is consequently criticized,
the wounded cries of *foul* reverberate through the hallowed
halls. Legislative honor has been questioned. Angry legislators rush to the defense of the wounded one; cries of *shame*
spring from their lips. A colleague's honor has been sullied. It
is the "in" thing to defend him.

Legislative honor is important. Of course, it is actually
nothing more than telling the truth, a custom to be encouraged
under all circumstances. But to think one's colleagues and
lobbyists respect this unwritten rule at all times is the height of
naiveté. In California as in most legislative halls, no senator or
assemblyman or witness now testifying before committee is
under oath. There is no placing of the hand on the Bible and
swearing to tell the truth, the whole truth and nothing but the
truth, so help me God, or going to jail if you lie.

All testimony, all debate is taken and presented as gospel
truth, and to question the veracity of the information is tantamount to questioning grandma's right to bake biscuits.
Rarely, however, does one run into a bald-faced lie. These
men are professionals and bald-faced lying is uncouth, ungentlemanly, and unnecessary. Through the gentle arts of omission, oration, and subtle persuasion, the whole, plain, ugly
truth can be artfully evaded. Once in a while, it is possible to
catch them with their verbal pants around their knees, but it is a
rare occasion. Even if it occurs, there is so such thing as
perjury before a committee. There are no punitive measures
that can be taken against one who will distort or misstate the
facts.

The more important the bill, the higher the stakes. Doesn't it stand to reason that the greater chances will be taken to guarantee its success? I know I'm a cad to imply that maybe the truth, the whole truth, and nothing but the truth is not always present at committee hearings all the time, but surely we can agree that an occasional teeny weeny fib or two or a teeny weeny omission may occur?

I am not trying to repeal lying. A lot of folks do it on occasion, but whenever Joe Citizen tells a whopper, it usually hurts only himself and those who have believed him. When a legislator tells one, it sometimes becomes law with the full force of government behind it. The wider the range of legislative action, the greater the chance of deception.

21

Sexy Solons

I WASN'T GOING to talk about sex in this book, but to discuss the legislators without at least one chapter on the subject would be like discussing the 1940's without mentioning World War II. As one well-known politician said, "legislators, lust you all."

Legislators are all too human and suffer the infirmities of other mortals, in fact, maybe more so because of the temptation put before them. A lot of girlies think latching onto a legislator is a real prize and the legislative halls have their share of groupies hoping to glom onto a sexy solon. Being a legislator is an ego trip for many and big egos and sex attract each other.

Many a marriage has been split asunder a short while after the local hero was elected. Many a wife has chosen to stay in the district rather than pull up stakes and travel to the Capital with her spouse. Sometimes it works out, especially if the legislative session is a short one, but if the hubby is away for extended periods of time, temptation expands proportionate to loneliness. There are always some sweet things around to comfort the lonely legislator and scratch whatever ego needs itching.

One of the most interesting paradoxes is that some guys are real swingers before they hit the capitol halls, and so fooling around with the dollies is no big surprise, nor big news. No one thinks much about the erotic antics of the fast zipper set. The press usually ignores them because they are running true to form. One such legislative leader would have a new sweetie on his arm about every night and would blatantly show up with his new lover at all of the local bistros. It became so commonplace that the only thing newsworthy could be if he showed up with wife.

On the other hand, a number of fairly straight guys get elected and if they were caught horsing around it could jeopardize their standings in their district. Divorces are messy during an election year. More than one legislator has tried to subtly fool around and has been seen by someone who delights in knowing that old sanctimonious is sacking out with some governmental groupie. Bedroom blackmail is still alive and well in the legislative halls of America.

It is pretty tough to vote against a colleague's pet promotion when he knows what pet you've been promoting. On more than one occasion I have skipped introducing constituents to legislators I have met in restaurants because the odds were three to one the lady they were escorting wasn't their wife.

Fidelity to one's frau is not a prerogative of any one party nor to one's political liberalism or conservatism. I know "conservatives" who would make a pass at a table if it had a skirt on it. One such "conservative" had the well-deserved reputation of being the biggest chaser in town. During his heyday he reportedly had three apartments in town with his wife in one, his secretary in another, and the third for any strays he would pick up during the week. He was the idol of all of the other playboys, especially for his endurance—he never seemed to wear down. His virility was the talk of all of the other lesser-grade Capitol Casanovas, especially among some of the more rambunctious lobbyists.

As the story goes, it was only a matter of time before the more venturesome lobbyists got together and appointed one of their own to inquire into the mysteries of the Senator's great agility with the ladies. "Senator (er, ah, smirk, smirk), how do you do it? Heh, heh, heh."

The senator knew exactly what the question implied. The senator was also a great jokester and wasn't about to let this upstart get off unscathed for his affrontery. In mock seriousness the senator looked all around to see if others could possibly overhear, then leaned forward and whispered, "China. I get it from China." The bewildered inquirer responded loudly, "China?" "Ssh! Ssh!" hissed the senator, "Not so loud! I get a shipment of virility pills from the Orient. I don't know what the hell's in them, but they make me feel like the chief sheik at a harem convention."

"No kiddin'?" exclaimed the lobbyist.

"Yeah," leered the senator. "Now I know why there's so damn many Chinamen."

"Heh, heh," responded the lobbyist. "Er, Senator . . . would you happen to have any extra pills, I thought . . ."

"God, no," hissed the sensuous solon, "I just have enough to last me until the next shipment arrives. I haven't a pill to spare." "Oh," sighed the dejected lobbyist.

"Tell you what," the legislator lowered his voice again, looked around, "next time I see my supplier, I'll ask him to increase the shipment, but I'll tell you, it will cost! Are you interested?"

"Interested! Do lovers love a waterbed? Of course I'm interested."

"Well, I'll ask, but don't count on anything. These pills are hard to get."

The senator strung the lobbyist out for months. The longer it took for the passion pills to arrive the more credible the story became to the lobbyist. By now he had told all of his acquaintances of the source of the senator's power and the number of those interested in the passion pills had increased dramatically. There was hardly a week that the senator wasn't approached by some new friend wanting to get in on the pills from Peking.

When the interest was at its height, the sensuous senator called in his lobbyist friends and announced, "Next week, my shipment will be in, and what's more, there will be extra pills available for all of you!''

Delight permeated the bars around the Capitol. God Eros would reign as long as the pills held out.

The senator collected the money in advance to pay for the shipment and with his pockets bulging with loot, he cornered a colleague, who in private life was a pharmacist.

"Charlie," asked the senator, "can you give me the name of some pill that is harmless but yet will do something to you that is memorable?''

"Sure, got just the thing . . . .''

"What does it do?''

"Nothing harmful, but when you go to the bathroom to wee wee, it comes out blue. One problem though, it stains anything it touches a bright blue and is difficult to remove.''

"Perfect!'' smirked the senator.

A few days later he dispensed the pills amidst a flurry of fervent thank you's to a number of grateful buyers. They in turn must have had subcontractors because over the next few days there was hardly a commode within six blocks of the capitol that wasn't stained a bright blue. Senator Sensuous had left his indelible mark upon the capitol.

I don't want to leave you with the feeling that all legislators are horking around on their wives . . . not so. There are some straight shooters in the legislature. The point is there are more opportunities to err placed before solons than before the average man on the street.

The morals of a legislator are more important than those of the average citizen because of the nature of the job. The legislature redistributes great wealth and regulates. It has power over other people's lives. The promiscuity of Joe Doakes down the block will have little effect upon your life, but the bedroom antics of your legislator could affect how he votes. The more power the public gives to the legislature, the greater the chance that someone is going to get screwed.

22

God Alone

THERE ARE a lot of utopians around who believe that the state is the vehicle to bring about the good life for all. Logic suggests the alternative; the state, when given arbitrary power to "do good things," will frequently oppress the very people it intends to help. Why? It's obvious. People aren't perfect, and, the last time I looked, people are the ones who run governments.

I've tried to show in the preceding chapters that legislators are all too human. We are subject to jealousy, self-interest, greed, petty dislikes, covetousness, mistakes, carnal desires, ego, vanity, impetuousness, dumbness, biased opinions, and a host of other human frailties. Because of the power that is condensed into our hands, these shortcomings are magnified.

When we legislators goof we can hurt hundreds of thousands of people—especially when we try to regulate human behavior while envisioning ourselves as the redistributors of wealth.

Governments of men are necessary to preserve the peace and protect our individual liberties from both foreign and domestic criminals. There are a lot of self-ordained political priests afloat in the sea of humanity, and all too often they collect together to rule governments—and destroy liberty in the process.

It would be wonderful if man were perfectible, but, alas, it will never be in this life. Perfectibility presupposes that imperfect man knows what perfection is and that an imperfect man is capable of implementing perfection. Man, for all of his capabilities, will always be a sow's ear. Human perfectibility is accomplishable only by God and by Him alone.

Is all of the aforementioned cause for despair? Of course not. Man's nature is flawed, but he is not without redeeming qualities. There are political circumstances where he can exist in relative peace with his fellow man, where his shortcomings can sometimes be used to everyone's advantage.

When such a limited government exists, our propensity to goof is restricted to those with whom we deal. Also, when our actions are positive, we are the immediate recipients of our own good judgment. When we do not look to the state as our benefactor, we have to look to ourselves. We must then offer services to others in order to survive. In interaction with others, antagonism, hatred, and animosity are unrewarding. Free men, by necessity, prefer more harmonious relationships, not necessarily because all *want* to be harmonious, but because it serves one's self-interest to do so.

Man wants. He desires goods and services that satisfy his material needs. If harmony is what provides these needs, he will keep in tune with the rest of the human choir.

Freedom creates a dynamic force. A complex society can only survive where man's talents are allowed to prosper, individual creativity is encouraged and rewarded, excellence is sought, and mediocrity is relegated to its proper station.

Will utopia arrive with freedom? Of course not. We still have to deal with those amongst us who would rather steal, cheat, groan, and moan. Freedom doesn't guarantee that all human suffering will be alleviated, but the odds are much better that man's overall lot will dramatically improve.

Freedom necessarily elevates the individual, and as the individual improves, society benefits as a whole. What else *is* society than a collection of individuals?

What's the answer? What is our hope? How about a nation and eventually a world of free people? I believe this is the destiny of future generations.

One need look only at the history of mankind to see the inevitability of human freedom. Man, in all of his dumbness, has been struggling upward—falling back from time to time, but ever so perceptibly advancing, painfully discovering the revealed truths of the nature of man.

One truth should now be evident. *Each* person has inalienable rights and government's role should be limited to the protection of personal freedom.

Unfortunately, America is now temporarily staggering backward, away from liberty. We are submerging into the warm goo of a paternalistic government and constricting our freedom of movement. In our all too human quest for security we are offering our personal freedom as the price.

Being free is heady business and sometimes frightening. But remember, if you overindulge in too much government and you are worried and upset, take a good dose of freedom. Try it. You'll like it.